Japanese Language & Culture

How to Discover the Ins and Outs of Japanese Society so that You Can Learn Japanese in the Right Way

Yuto Kanazawa

© Copyright – All Rights Reserved

The content contained within this book may not be reproduced, duplicated or transmitted without direct written permission from the author or the publisher.

Under no circumstances will any blame or legal responsibility be held against the publisher, or author, for any damages, reparation, or monetary loss due to the information contained within this book, either directly or indirectly.

Legal Notice:

This book is copyright protected. It is only for personal use. You cannot amend, distribute, sell, use, quote or paraphrase any part, or the content within this book, without the consent of the author or publisher.

Disclaimer Notice:

Please note the information contained within this document is for educational and entertainment purposes only. All effort has been executed to present accurate, up to date, reliable, complete information. No warranties of any kind are declared or implied. Readers acknowledge that the author is not engaged in the rendering of legal, financial, medical or professional advice. The content within this book has been derived from various sources. Please consult a licensed professional before attempting any techniques outlined in this book.

By reading this document, the reader agrees that under no circumstances is the author responsible for any losses, direct or indirect, that are incurred as a result of the use of the information contained within this document, including, but not limited to, errors, omissions, or inaccuracies.

Table of Contents

Introduction	5
Chapter 1 Origins of Etiquette in Japan	7
The Samurai	7
The Social System	8
Harmony	10
Chapter 2 Etiquette in Language	11
Pronunciation	11
Proper Use of Names	18
Proper Use of Titles	19
Name Cards	21
Useful Phrases and Words	24
Etiquette of Conversing	26
The Art of Bowing	28
How to Shake Hands	38
Chapter 3 The Importance of the Group	40
'Cold' Introductions	42
Chapter 4 Going Out	44
Seating	44
Dining and Eating	47
Drinking in Japan	54
Public Etiquette	60
Chapter 5 Praise and Criticism	69

Chapter 6 Visiting Shrines and Temples	71
Shinto Shrine Etiquette	72
Buddhist Temple Etiquette	76
Chapter 7 Visiting Another's Home	80
Chapter 8 Bathroom Etiquette:	85
Public Bathrooms	85
Finding Public Bathrooms	85
Types of Toilets and How to Use Them	87
Public Bathroom Etiquette	88
Private or Hotel Bathrooms	89
Hotel Bathrooms	89
Private Bathrooms	89
Private or Hotel Bathroom Etiquette	90
Bathing and Showering in Japan	90
Bathing and Showering Etiquette	91
Chapter 9 Staying at Hotels	92
Chapter 10 Japanese Ceremonies and Festivals	95
Japanese Festivals	95
Japanese Tea Ceremony	98
Tea Ceremony Etiquette	98
Conclusion	103

Introduction

Etiquette is described as the rules that a society must follow in order to ensure that the correct behavior and manners that are expected of a person are shown. Etiquette is seen as a code of conduct for members of a society to follow. In Japan, etiquette is more than a set of rules or a code of conduct. It is their way of life. There are many countries around the world that too have their own form of etiquette, but the role of etiquette in Japan became so important that this behavior became the law of the land and took precedence over almost everything including reason and human feeling.

There are many things that helped to form the etiquette that we see in modern Japan, from the role the military played to even the myths and legends of Japan's creation. There are also many things that the etiquette in Japan relied on to stay relevant, such as the social system and the role of harmony. It took a lot to build the country that Japan is today, and they are not about to let their way of life change any time soon.

Japan is one of the most mannered countries in the world. Their society is built on respect and harmony, and each individual member of society works with other members to keep the balance. Unfortunately, this kind of life has left the Japanese extremely sensitive to any culture but their own, and they are often guarded against beliefs and thoughts of outsiders. This makes it very difficult for anyone who doesn't know the culture and etiquette of Japan to be welcomed into the country and enjoy its beauty and wonder. It is especially difficult for businessmen and big companies to find a foothold in Japan.

Japan is closed off to outsiders, but that won't be a problem for you if you learn to become an insider. If you learn their culture, rules of society, and way of life, you will be welcomed into their country with open arms. It is highly recommended that anyone wishing to visit Japan take a moment to familiarize themselves with the dos and don'ts of their society. Once you know the etiquette of Japan, you will be able to enjoy more deeply the wonder and beauty of the culture and the country.

Chapter 1

Origins of Etiquette in Japan

Japan's history is unique to that of any other country. It is long, blighted by conflicts, and filled with many fantastical tales of gods and deities. Buried inside the history of Japan, you will find the origins of its etiquette. There are mixed views on where modern-day Japan's etiquette actually came from. How and when did this system begin? What was it that formed Japan into the most mannered country in the world today?

One tale of the origins of etiquette revolves around the native Shinto religion. Shinto translates into "way of the gods." This religion is a kind of nature worship. Those who follow Shintoism believe that all things, including trees, rocks, rivers, and such are not mindless, lifeless things but are alive and have spirits. These spirits are deserving of a certain degree of respect and honor. To ensure that none of these spirits, seen or unseen, are disrespected or treated incorrectly in any way, the Japanese developed a way of life that has always been well mannered and respectful. This attitude they held towards the unseen spirits of the world helped to shape the way they live and act today.

The Samurai

Japanese etiquette was formalized between 1336 and 1573, which is the Muromachi age. This is the period of their history that saw the rise of the samurai and the military class. The Ogasawara clan, a respected samurai caste, was responsible for an anthology known as, "The Three Unified Teachings." This teaching included archery, horsemanship, and etiquette and served as a code for the samurai class. Their form of etiquette ensured safety around other fighting men by signaling no malicious intent through their mannerisms and movements. This required the samurai to have perfect movement as the smallest mistake in movement or posture could signal malicious intent and was dangerous.

The samurai were the only people allowed to carry weapons and hold office. They followed Zen Buddhism as their own form of religion and developed a lifestyle centered on loyalty to their masters and the use of a sword. Their lifestyle that came with constant and strict mental and physical discipline not only made them one of the most feared warriors in the world but also the most mannered group of people.

Back then, the samurai were very high up in society and they had a lot of power. Unfortunately, this led to many of them becoming arrogant and they ended up abusing their power. They were quick to give out harsh punishments for the smallest of things. The samurai very rarely needed to look to a higher authority for permission to do anything. This is what made the common people and lower classes so obedient. They went through great lengths to ensure that the samurai were not angered and had no reason to deal out punishment. Through this, the lower classes developed their own form of etiquette towards the higher classes and the samurai which would play a role in modern etiquette in Japan today.

This etiquette was only taught to the samurai class and to nobility up until the Edo period. Until this period, etiquette was seen as a skill that could save a life and had a masculine quality. However, after the Edo period, the lower classes of society, like the merchant class, had enough money to study etiquette. Once the lower classes were able to learn this etiquette, it was no longer seen as a life-saving skill but instead as an affectation of the leisure classes. The lower classes of society saw it more as a strict protocol or a rigid form of mannerism.

The Social System

The social system in Japan, also known as the vertical society, is a rigid system of classes. People in Japan are divided into classes of power and privilege, which is arranged in a vertical pattern with the most powerful and privileged classes at the top and the least at the bottom. This system ruled Japan since the beginning. The vertical society played a huge role in Japan's etiquette. Specific kinds of behavior and manners were expected from the different levels of the society. This was required to maintain the differences in class and keep those in power feeling powerful. It helped feed the vanity of the higher levels and kept the lower levels in check.

The development of Japan's social system is attributed to that of ancient China, as the Japanese borrowed many things from China and their social systems are extremely similar. However, the origin of the vertical society may have been caused by the belief that certain families in Japan were considered more divine and godly than others. This belief comes from the myth of the creation of Japan.

According to this myth, Izanami and Izanagi, a god and goddess, gave birth to the Japanese islands. The god and goddess were so enchanted by the beauty of the islands they had created that they descended from the heavens in order to live on these islands. The myth tells about how the Japanese are the direct descendants of lesser gods that also came to live on the islands. From the very beginning of Japan's history, the ruling class was believed to be direct descendants of these gods and they ruled in the god's names. Japan's leaders and emperors were directly related to these gods and so they were seen and treated as gods themselves. For this reason, the leaders always took their place at the very top of the vertical society and those that fell below the leader were descendants of lesser gods or were considered not to be the descendants of gods at all but the descendants of those who were related to gods.

The emperor was seated on top of the pyramid followed by members of the royal family. Then court officials and priests; members of the military or samurai fell underneath them, and they were followed by scholars and artisans. At the very bottom of the pyramid you would find the farmers and the merchants.

Although this vertical society was eventually broken down by law, it has still been etched into the history of Japan. Most who live there are used to this social system and still live with it and by it. The vertical society system can even be seen in a Japanese family, with the oldest members of the family holding the most power and demanding the most respect and the youngest members of the family being the most submissive and less important.

Harmony

One of the foundations of the social system in Japan was the role of harmony, or "wa." The role of harmony in society is basically the practice that every individual is required to do exactly what is expected of him in the exact manner it needs to be done. If every individual does what is expected of him or her, no more or less, then the harmony of the society is kept in balance. This system called for absolute harmony among people and between people and gods. This of course required everyone to follow the social system and accept the structure of the society.

Harmony in all behavior and relationships, professional, personal, and in public, took precedence over everything including human feelings. It required a controlled form of etiquette from each individual. Even though this system of harmony is not as strict today as it once was, anyone would tell you that "wa" still remains the building block for Japan's society.

The importance of the role of harmony is pretty straightforward; it removed the element of surprise from their society. If everyone did exactly what was expected of them then there were no surprises. Life was harmonious because it was predictable. This led to a sort of telepathic ability for the Japanese as they were able to predict reactions and responses from others to the point where any kind of verbal communication wasn't even necessary.

The role Japanese etiquette plays today is so important that it has left the Japanese very sensitive to any other way of life. Western culture in particular can be dramatically different, and it can be difficult for both cultures to work together without misunderstanding.

Chapter 2

Etiquette in Language

There is certain etiquette in the Japanese language. Some of this may be hard to see or even understand. Language is a sensitive thing for the Japanese and there are many things that come together to form their language. There is a certain way to speak and engage with one another. Body language is also part of this. There is a way you must hold yourself in public or in the company of others. There is the correct way to shake someone's hand or bow to them and there is an incorrect way of doing so. You must pronounce someone's name a certain way and use the correct titles when addressing them. All of these things, and more, work together to form the delicate language of etiquette in Japan.

Pronunciation

Japanese is based on five vowels that are combined with a number of consonants that create syllables. These syllables are then combined together to form various words. On the surface, Japanese seems like a pretty simple language. However, the only simple part about this language is learning to pronounce the various syllables properly.

If you plan on visiting Japan, then you probably don't need to go as far as learn to speak the language in its entirety. Learning to pronounce these syllables correctly could make your trip there a little easier. If you are a foreigner, you will most likely be forgiven for incorrectly pronouncing a phrase, word, or name. However, there are some cases where mispronouncing a simple phrase can lead to a huge misunderstanding. It's better to be safe by knowing how to pronounce things correctly.

A, I, U, E, and O, are the Roman letters used to represent the five vowels in Japanese.

A is pronounced like the 'a' in father, (ah.)

I is pronounced like the 'I' in ink, (ee.)

U is pronounced like the 'u' in rue, (uu.)

E is pronounced like the 'e' in leopard, (eh.)

O is pronounced like the 'o' in boo, (oh.)

These five vowels are then added at the end of several consonants to make a syllable. These syllables make up the entirety of the Japanese language. What follows is a list of the syllables in the Japanese language along with the correct way to pronounce them. If you follow these pronunciations like you would in English, then they will sound how they should in Japanese.

The Primary Syllables:

Ka pronounced kah.

Ki pronounced kee.

Ku pronounced kuu.

Ko pronounced koe.

Sa pronounced sah.

Shi pronounced she.

Su pronounced sue.

Se pronounced say.

So pronounced so.

Ta pronounced tah.

Chi pronounced chee.

Tsu pronounced t'sue.

Te pronounced tay.

To pronounced toe.

Na pronounced nah.

Ni pronounced nee.

Nu pronounced nuu.

Ne pronounced nay.

No pronounced no.

Ha pronounced hah.

Hi pronounced hee.

Hu pronounced who.

He pronounced hay.

Ho pronounced hoe.

Ma pronounced mah.

Mi pronounced me.

Mu pronounced moo.

Me pronounced may.

Mo pronounced moe.

Ya pronounced yah.

I pronounced ee.

Yu pronounced yuu.

E pronounced eh.

Yo pronounced yoe.

Ra pronounced rah.

Ri pronounced ree.

Ru pronounced rue.

Re pronounced ray.

Ro pronounced roe.

Ga pronounced gah.

Gi pronounced ghee.

Gu pronounced goo.

Ge pronounced gay.

Go pronounced go.

Za pronounced zah.

Zi pronounced jee.

Zu pronounced zoo.

Ze pronounced zay.

Zo pronounced zoe.

Da pronounced dah.

Ji pronounced jee.

De pronounced day.

Do pronounced doe.

Ba pronounced bah.

Bi pronounced bee.

Bu pronounced boo.

Be pronounced bay.

Bo pronounced boe.

Pa pronounced pah.

Pi pronounced pee.

Pu pronounced puu.

Pe pronounced pay.

Po pronounced poe.

(Important note: the syllables Ji and Zi sound basically the same when pronouncing them.)

(Important note: the letter R in the Japanese language is pronounced similar to the letter L in the English language. The R's are also rolled a little bit when you are saying a Japanese word.)

Combined Syllables:

These are syllables in the Japanese language, but they are a combination of two of the syllables in the list above. These syllables are seen as one syllable and pronounced as one, not two. When two syllables are combined, their spelling is changed slightly. Bi and Yu are put together to form the syllable Byu.

Rya pronounced re-yah.

Ryu pronounced re-yuu.

Ryo pronounced re-yoe.

Mya pronounced me-yah.

Myu pronounced me-yuu.

Myo pronounced me-yoe.

Nya pronounced ne-yah.

Nyu pronounced ne-yuu.

Nyo pronounced ne-yoe.

Hya pronounced he-yah.

Hyu pronounced he-yuu.

Hyo pronounced he-yoe.

Cha pronounced chah.

Chu pronounced chuu.

Cho pronounced choe.

Sha pronounced shah.

Shu pronounced shuu.

Sho pronounced show.

Kya pronounced q'yah.

Kyu pronounced que.

Kyo pronounced q'yoe.

Pya pronounced p'yah.

Pyu pronounced p'yuu.

Pyo pronounced p'yoe.

Bya pronounced b'yah.

Byu pronounced b'yuu.

Byo pronounced b'yoe.

Ja pronounced jah.

Ju pronounced juu.

Jo pronounced joe.

Gya pronounced g'yah.

Gyu pronounced g'yuu.

Gyo pronounced g'yoe.

(Important note: There are no L or V sounds in the Japanese language which is why there are no syllables containing them. Most Japanese, when they try to pronounce an English word with either of these letters will use B instead of V and R instead of L. In others words they would pronounce the word "very" as "bery.")

(Important note: The letters G and H in Japanese have a very hard pronunciation, like in the words go and ho.)

(Important note: There are long vowels in Japanese which should be pronounced twice as long as the normal vowel. These long vowels will have a line above them.)

(Important note: Sometimes the vowels I and U are weak in pronunciation. In other words the word desu, which means 'to be,' is pronounced dess.)

It seems complicated, but there are simple ways that can help. It is easier to pronounce a word if you break it down to the syllables that make it up. Arigato, which is Japanese for 'thank you,' can be broken down into four syllables; a-ri-ga-to. Now all you have to do is pronounce each syllable the English way shown in the lists above. Arigato is pronounced ah-ree-gah-toe. You see it's actually quite simple. Practicing pronouncing each syllable will help you immensely when it comes to pronounced names, titles, and simple phrases while visiting Japan.

Proper Use of Names

Depending on what part of the world you are from, you probably use someone's first name when talking to or about them. In Japan it is a bit more complicated than that. A part of Japanese etiquette involves the restriction of using someone's given name even in social and intimate situations. The Japanese would rather use someone's last name, though in modern Japan, it is usually only the adults that follow this custom.

When adults are greeting or conversing with each other, they tend to use each other's last names. This is seen as a more formal and appropriate way to converse. However, children usually use each other's first names in any situation. Children also tend to refer to each other by nicknames, shortened versions of their first names, and their family names depending on their relationship and level of friendship. When children grow up, they tend to change their ways and start referring to each other by their last names. Even adults who have known each other all their life will use each other's last name when conversing. This is true even today. When two people are dating, they would usually use each other's first names, or they would use a diminutive of their first name. This is also true among family members and close friends. Parents also refer to their children by their first names.

Japanese first names are usually made up of two or more syllables and they can be challenging to remember and pronounce. To make this easier, the Japanese use diminutives of first names. Diminutives are usually only common among family members and extremely close friends. A diminutive of someone's name usually takes the first or the first two syllables of someone's name and adds the word 'chan,' pronounced chahn, at the end. Adding chan at the end of someone's name is the equivalent of shortening someone's name in English, like saying Alex instead of Alexandra. Here are some examples of common Japanese names and their diminutives:

Tomoko would be Tomo-chan, (toe-moe-chahn.)

Kiyoshi would be Ki-chan, (kee-chahn.)

The word chan can be added to a baby's and child's name by their parents and other adults. Children can do the same with their siblings, parents, grandparents, and friends. When you are visiting Japan, it will be acceptable for you to address children and babies in this way.

Young dating couples will usually refer to each other by their first names or use diminutives, but this usually changes once they get older and are married. In the past, husbands would refer to their wives as kimi (kee-me) or o-mae (oh-my,) both of which can be translated as "you." Wives would refer to their husbands as anata (ah-nah-tah,) which can be translated as "dear." When they had children, the husband would refer to his wife as o-ka-san (oh-kaahsahn,) which can be translated as "mother" or "mama." After having children, the wife would refer to her husband as o-to-san (oh-toe-sahn,) which can be translated as "father" or "papa." This way of thinking has changed slightly over the years and nowadays husbands and wives may refer to each other by their first names. However, after having children, they will still refer to each other as "mother" and "father."

This strict view on using names in Japan is slowly changing and becoming more Americanized. It's becoming more socially acceptable to use the first name of a close friend or even the first name of an acquaintance. However, to be on the safe side, it's better if you refer to other adults by their last names or their titles during your trip to Japan, unless you have been told that you can do otherwise. If in a business situation, it is always better to use last names or titles.

Proper Use of Titles

One of the key factors of Japan's vertical society was the use of titles instead of names. Titles would separate classes and groups in order to keep the balance and relationship between the different levels of the social system. Today, the use of titles instead of names is still as important as it used to be. Using titles to address someone is mostly used when visiting public places like the grocery store or a business.

Here are some examples of everyday titles you may hear or have to use:

Butcher or "Mr. Meat Man" would be Nikuya-san (nee-kuu-yah-sahn.)

Bartender would be Ba-tenda (bah-tane-dah.)

Buddhist would be O-Bo-san (oh-boh-sahn.)

Cook would be Kuuk-san (cook-sahn.)

Carpenter or "Mr. Carpenter" would be Daiku-san (dike-sahn)

Customer, visitor, or guest, or "Mr. Guest" and "Mr. Customer" would be O-Kyaku-san (Oh-kyack-sahn,) or (oh-kyack-sah-mah,) which is the more polite version and can be used on both men and women.

Policeman would be O-Mawari-san (oh-mah-wah-ree-sahn)

Driver or "Mr. Driver" would be Untenshu-san (uun-ten-shoe-sahn,) this can be for a driver of a taxi or a private car.

Doctor or "Mr. Doctor" would be O-isha-san (oh-ee-shah-sahn)

Waiter would be Weta (way-tah)

Waitress would be Wetoresu (way-toe-ray-suu)

Postman would be Yubinya-san (yuu-bean-yah-sahn)

Train conductor would be Shasho-san (shah-show-sahn)

School principle would be KM-cho sensei (Kohh-chohh sen-say-e)

Senior in school, or work would be Senpai (sen-pie)

Young women or "Miss Young Lady," (usually used for single women,) would be o-jo-san (oh-joe-sahn)

Your wife would be Oku-san (oak-sahn)

Your husband would be Go-shujin (go-shuu-jeen)

Shinto Priest would be Kannushi-san (kahn-nuu-she-sahn)

The use of titles instead of names is especially important in Japanese business. Here are some examples of titles you may use in business situations in Japan:

President would be Shacho (shah-choe)

Chairman of the Board would be Kaicho (kye-choe)

Vice president would be Fuku-shacho (fuu-kuu-shah-choe)

Senior executive managing director would be Senmu (sem-muu)

Executive managing director would be Jomu (joe-muu)

Supervisor would be Kakari-cho (kah-kah-ree-choe)

Section manager would be Kacho (kah-choe)

Department manager or just the general manager would be Bucho (buu-choe)

Deputy general or department manager would be Bucho Dairi (buu-choe die-ree)

Deputy manager would be Dairi (die-ree)

Deputy section manager would be Kacho Dairi (kah-choe die-ree)

It's not that important for a tourist to learn to use business titles during their visit in Japan. However, if you do need to use them, you will be respected if you do use them properly. This will also help you get your point across quickly and easily. It also makes life simpler when you need to address someone without knowing their last or even first name: a title is always accepted.

Name Cards

Name cards are used a lot in Japan, mostly in the business world in official situations. They are seen as an important part of Japanese culture and etiquette. The use of name cards wasn't seen in Japan until about the 1870's when the last samurai clan put down their swords and Japan began to industrialize. Today, name cards are used mostly in the business world to help an individual quickly and simply determine someone's title. By knowing someone's title, you would in turn know their social rank and the amount of respect due to them. Before the introduction of name cards, the Japanese had other ways to determine these factors at a glance.

Back in early Japan, the vertical society separated the classes and had some groups ranking higher, socially, than other groups. When someone was in a higher social standing than you, they were due a certain amount of respect from you. If you weren't sure of someone's social rank it was best to avoid any meeting with them. You wouldn't want to assume they were on the same level as you and give them the wrong amount of respect. In some cases, being unable to show someone the proper amount of respect that was due to them could even mean death if you got it wrong. Prior to 1868, the Meiji Restoration period, there were often visible factors that would help you determine an individual's social ranking.

Clothing and family crests used to be one surefire way of knowing someone's social ranking upon first glance. Each class in the vertical society and in some occupations had a distinctive uniform to wear. Some of these uniforms were required by law. For instance, the style or the kimono a man wore would indicate his position in the social ranking. Also, the style of a woman's kimono would indicate her marital status and her age. This was an easy way for people to determine the social ranking of the people around them and the amount of respect that they were due.

If people didn't want to form a relationship with a stranger, then they would simply avoid them at a safe distance or with indifference when distance was not an option. However, if they did want to form a relationship or one was unavoidable for work reasons, this system of determining rank easily was extremely helpful. At a glance you could determine someone's position in the social system, and you could introduce yourself accordingly, using the perfect amount of respect from the beginning.

Japan is a very different country today. There have been massive changes in government, and the feudalistic clans have all been abolished. However, the country has been conditioned to act and treat each other a certain way for thousands of years. Just because the vertical society doesn't exist anymore, it doesn't mean people are going to act as if it doesn't. Today they still believe in a social ranking and a degree of respect that is due to those in a certain rank. Therefore, the importance of knowing someone's title and social ranking is still there. Name cards came in handy for this reason. You could hand someone your name card and receive theirs in return. Then both of you will know each other's title and social ranking from the get-go and there would be no chance of disrespecting one another accidentally.

You may not need to hand out a name card if you are just visiting Japan as they are mostly used in the business world. However, if you are visiting Japan for business reasons, I would suggest printing out a few name cards. Have someone translate your name and title into Romanized Japanese syllables and then have them printed on the reverse side of your name cards. It's important that you get the translation of your name right because sometimes native Japanese speakers will have difficulty reading and pronouncing an English name.

When giving your card to someone, there is certain etiquette you need to follow. First, directly face the person you're giving the card to while holding your card with both hands, the Japanese side facing up. Then, extend both your arms out and hand them the card with a smile and a slight bow of the head. As you take the other person's card, tell them your name along with some kind of polite greeting. For example, "My name is John. I am pleased to meet you." You can say this in English, or if you know how to say it in Japanese then do so.

Once you have the other person's card, look at the name and title on the card immediately. This will help you to determine whether or not this person is below or above you on the social rank and you can bow accordingly. If they are your senior, then a tradition bow at the waist at a 45-degree angle should be the right amount of respect. If they are below you and you have no reason to cater to them, then your bow can be shorter and shallower.

When you are exchanging cards with multiple people, it is considered rude to rush the process. Politely hand out your card to each person one by one as you would if you were only handing it out to one person. Also, keep your cards neatly packed in a leather or plastic holder. This will protect the cards from getting damaged and it will look a little bit more professional. It is also rude to hand out name cards that are less than perfect in condition.

Try to take notice of the mannerisms of the people around you. Japan is changing, and with the newer generation taking charge, these formal customs have become less formal. There may be no need for name cards, or you may not need to hand them out in such a strict and formal way. You will be able to tell straight away from the way someone is acting whether or not you need to be as formal. Some people won't require such a high level of etiquette from you.

Useful Phrases and Words

When you're visiting another country, it isn't necessary to learn a whole different language. However, it can be helpful to learn a few words and phrases in that language. You should learn words like 'hello' and 'help me.' When learning Japanese words and phrases, it is important to know that most words and phrases in Japanese have a formal and informal pronunciation. A certain phrase, such as good morning, will have a formal and informal way to say it. Both ways are polite, but one is seen as more polite than the other. During your trip to Japan, you may be exposed to formal situations. All of the following words and phrases should be widely accepted in most of these situations.

Greetings:

Hello = Konnichiwa (this can also be used to say "Good Afternoon")

Good Morning = Ohayou Gozaimas

Good Evening = Konbanwa

Goodbye = Sayonara

See you later = Ja matane

Simple Conversation:

Please = Kudasai

Thank you = Arigato Gozaimas (for extremely informal situations just use "Arigato")

How are you? = O Genki Des Ka

I'm Fine, Thanks = Hai, Genki Des

Excuse me or Sorry = Sumimasen

Yes = Hai

No = Iie

My name is = Watashi no namae wa...*your name*...des

I'd like = O Kudasai (this is the polite way to ask for a food item when eating out)

The Bill, Please = Okaikei wo onegaishimas

I don't understand = Wakarimasen

Help! = Tasukete!

Questions:

How much is this? = Ikura desu ka?

What is this? = Kore wa nan desu ka?

Do you accept credit cards? = Kurejitto kaado wa tsukaemas ka?

Can you speak English? = Eigo wa hanasemas ka?

Where is the toilet? = Toire wa do ko desu ka?

Can you translate this for me? = Yakushite kudasai?

Simple Numbers:

1 = Ichi

2 = Ni

3 = San

4 = Yon

5 = Go

6 = Roku

7 = Nana

8 = Hachi

9 = Kyuu

10 = Juu

These few phrases, words, and numbers should help you navigate and communicate while in Japan, even if you don't speak any Japanese.

Etiquette of Conversing

There are certain conversational rules we follow in our cultures. They're often not explicitly stated, but we know them very well and following the rules shows respect. In Japan the same rules apply, only their rules are a little different. There is a certain way to speak in Japan that is respectful and accepted. There are only a few rules to keep in mind when conversing with someone in Japan whether you are in a formal or an informal situation.

Nod Your Head:

It may seem silly, but an important part of the Japanese language, both verbal and physical, is nodding your head. During a conversation with someone, it is very important to nod your head while you are listening to them talk. This will show them that you are paying attention to them and that you understand what they are telling you. This is true whether they are speaking in Japanese or in English. It's one of the most important rules of speaking with someone in Japan.

You Don't Need to Talk:

Remaining silent is an expected form of non-verbal communication in Japan. You don't have to fill the silence with chatter. Don't feel the need to chat just because the silence feels awkward or uncomfortable. Silence is natural and it is accepted and expected in some situations.

On the same subject of talking to someone, try not to interrupt someone else while they are speaking. Wait till they are finished then say what you need to.

Don't Stand Too Close:

You can't stand too close to someone in Japan. For many reasons, the Japanese like to have their personal space. As a rule of thumb, keep a bowing distance or an arm's length between you and someone else.

Don't show any affection to someone else while out in public. You may be allowed to hug or kiss a close friend or partner, but avoid doing this in public. It is considered rude to show this type of affection while out in public.

Don't Point:

Pointing with one finger is seen as a rude and threatening gesture in Japan. If you need to point out an object or point in a certain direction, there is a correct way to do it. The Japanese point with their four fingers in the direction but with their fingers pressed together and their thumb folded into their palm. Never point at someone in this way or any other way. You should only point in this way at objects or in directions.

Beckoning:

The Japanese do not beckon people with their forefingers. This is similar to pointing and is seen as rude or threatening. To beckon someone, extend your arm out fully in front of you, bend your wrist down, and wave your fingers back and forth keeping them pressed tightly together. Do not beckon people who are older than you or with a higher-ranking status.

Sitting:

Sitting out in public might seem like a simple thing that you can't get wrong, but you can. It's better to sit with your back and neck straight and with both your feet flat on the floor. Never sit with your one ankle on your knee.

Don't Shake Your Head:

When you want to say "no" to someone or say that you don't understand, don't shake your head. This is seen as impolite. It is polite to wave your hand back and forth in front of your face with your palm forward. This is a polite way to say things like "no," "I don't know," or "I don't understand."

Be Punctual:

The Japanese greatly appreciate punctuality and arriving on time is a must for certain formal and even informal events. Arriving late will not be taken lightly, but you must also be careful of arriving too early.

The Art of Bowing

The act of bowing is hardwired into the Japanese culture and way of life. When most Japanese bow to one another in situations, they aren't even thinking about it, they're just doing it. In fact, if you asked someone from Japan when and how you should bow, they might find it hard to answer you. In some ways, the Japanese don't expect a tourist to bow to them in any situation. They understand that most foreigners won't understand their customs, so if you don't bow or if you bow incorrectly, you will likely be easily forgiven. However, if you were to bow in the correct way, you can ensure that you will earn yourself some points with the locals.

Bowing in Japan probably started somewhere between 538 and 794 AD during the Asuka and Nara periods. This was during the introduction of Chinese Buddhism into their culture. Bowing back then was used as a reflection of status and positioning in the vertical society. If you were of a lower class and you met someone of a higher status than you then you would bow to them. You would bow to put yourself in a vulnerable position and in effect succumb to the person of higher social standing. The more power the person has, the deeper you would bow to show more respect much like in the movies when someone would get on their knees and bow until their forehead touches the floor in front of the emperor.

Some of the old Japanese bowing customs have survived until modern times. Now, it is more of a friendly gesture of mutual respect and harmony. In modern Japan the act of bowing serves many different purposes. You would do it when you are;

1. Saying hello

2. Saying goodbye

3. Saying thank you

4. Congratulating someone

5. Apologizing

6. Starting a meeting, ceremony, or class

7. Ending a meeting, ceremony, or class

8. Worshipping something or someone

9. Asking someone for something

These are the basic occasions you will be required to bow to someone, but there are more instances when you would use a bow. Bowing isn't just an occasional act. Bowing is often used to convey certain emotions such as;

1. Respect

2. Appreciation

3. Remorse

4. Gratitude

There are plenty more emotions shown by bowing but the main one is respect. It is still true today that the deeper your bow the more respect you are showing someone. Also, the longer you bow the more respect you are showing.

The Basics of a Bow

Bowing can be very complicated or it can be quite basic if you take the time to learn the dos and don'ts of it. As a tourist and visitor in Japan, you may only be expected to know the simple things about bowing. Let's start with bowing positions. There are only two different positions from which you will perform a bow:

Sitting

Standing

These positions depend on the formality of the situation. Most extremely formal situations, such as ceremonies, will require a sitting bow and most informal situations will require a standing bow.

The Seated Bow:

There are a few types of different bows you can perform from a seated position. First, before you can perform any of these bows, you must know the correct sitting position from which to perform a bow. This sitting position is called seiza.

To start any of these bows you must first kneel down on the floor. Men should kneel down one knee at a time and women should place both knees down at the same time, if it is possible. The tops of your feet should be flat on the ground and your toes must be pointed straight behind you. You can rest your behind on your calves and keep your spine and neck as straight as possible. Your arms must remain at your sides with your hands resting palm-down on your thighs. This is the simple sitting position from which you will perform both bows and it is also the way you will be expected to sit in formal and maybe even informal situations.

I would suggest practicing sitting in this position as it can be very strenuous over long periods of time.

The Greeting Bow:

To perform this bow, also known as the seiza bow, start in the sitting position explained above. Start by bending forward at a 15-degree angle. Move at a natural pace, not too slow or too fast. While bowing forward, move your hands on your thighs towards the outside of your knees. Start sliding your hands at the same time as bowing your upper body and move them at the same pace. Place the tips of your fingers so you are lightly touching the ground in front of you. Make sure your hands are in line with your body. Keep your gaze downwards and hold for a few seconds. Return to the sitting position by reversing the actions that brought you forward and at the same pace you bowed forward.

You don't have to hold this bow for any specific period of time and you aren't required to move at a certain pace. However, you don't want to feel or look as if you are rushing through the bow. Don't linger but don't rush.

The Senrei "Polite" Bow:

The senrei bow is seen as the "polite bow." It's mostly used in semi-formal sitting situations where you wish to show a moderate amount of respect or gratitude. This is the most common sitting bow you will be performing.

Bend your upper body forward at a 30-degree angle over a one-second time frame and slide your hands forward towards your knees at the same pace and time. Men must place their hands palm down on the floor in front of their knees, about 3 cm apart. Women must place only the tips of their fingers on the ground in front of their knees with their thumbs touching each other. Your gaze must be directed at the floor in front of you. Only hold this position for about a second then return to a seated position at the same pace you bowed forward.

This bow sounds as though it looks rushed, but it is meant to look sincere and graceful. Take some time to practice this bow and ensure it does look this way and not rushed.

The Seated Respect Bow:

This is usually used in formal situations when you are wanting to show a moderate amount of respect to someone of a higher ranking than you. For example, you will perform this bow when in the presence of your boss or your in-laws. An important thing to remember is that unless you are already in sitting position, you don't need to perform this bow. If you are standing when greeting someone of a higher ranking, then performing a respectful standing bow is good enough.

While in the sitting position, bend your upper body forward until your forehead is about 30 cm from the floor in front of you. Your bend forward should take place over the span of 2.5 seconds. Place your hands flat on the floor in front of your making a triangle by placing the tips of your thumbs and forefingers together. Move your hands forward at the same time and speed as your bow forward. Hold your elbows slightly off the ground and your upper arms must be kept close to your body. Your gaze must be directed toward your index fingers. Hold this position for at least 3 seconds and return to the sitting position over the span of 4 seconds.

Chair Bow:

You may be sitting in a chair at a dinner table or in a meeting and it will still be required of you to bow. Some people will usually stand up and bow but this can be seen as quite formal. For informal chair bowing simply bow your upper body forward leaving some space between your back and the back of the chair. Women should keep their knees and feet together and men should keep their knees and feet apart by about 15 or 20 cm. In this situation, the bowing angles are usually the same as with standing bows.

The Standing Bow:

Standing bows in Japan are far more complicated than a seated bow. There are far more different ways to bow while standing. Every type of bow signals a different feeling or level of respect. I'll explain the most important bows you will need to know as a tourist.

The basic standing position for bowing is called seiritsu. For this position, you must stand up straight and look at a spot about 18 feet straight ahead of you. Men will keep their feet at least 3 cm apart while women should make sure their feet and knees are touching. Hands are placed lightly on the thighs at a diagonal angle. There should be a slight gap between your body and your elbows. Remember to breathe with your chest to help keep your body straight and centered. While standing in this position, you are ready to perform almost all standing bows.

The Nod Bow or Non-Bow:

This type of bow is usually quite informal and is used when dealing with close friends or relatives. If you have known someone for very long and you are quite close with them, then a full on bow isn't really necessary with them. That is where the nod bow or the non-bow comes in.

With this bow you will only need to incline your head forward slightly. You can keep your gaze on the person you're bowing to or you can direct your gaze at the floor for a moment. This is a very informal way to show respect and is often only used with very close friends or relatives. Make sure the person you are bowing to is okay with this type of bow before using it. Even if you have known them for a long time and you are really close, they may still prefer a more formal bow.

Eshaku the Greeting Bow:

This bow is usually used in situations when you are dealing with someone of the same social or business rank. This will be a friend of a friend or even a coworker. In these situations, you will perform the eshaku bow.

To start, stand in the seiritsu position and bend your upper body forward at a 15-degree angle. Do this at a natural pace, don't move too fast or too slow. Lower your hands about 3 to 4 cm down at the front of your legs at the same time and pace as your upper body. Your hands will be somewhere around the middle of your thighs while you're in the bowing position. Make sure to keep your gaze in line with your body and look at a spot about 6 feet in front of you. Stand up from this bow at the same pace you moved into it.

The Respect Bow:

This bow is usually known as the futsurei or keirei bow. This is a bow used to show more respect to someone. This bow is usually used on someone of a higher-ranking status than you or with someone who has some kind of power over you. In other words, you would use this bow on your boss or perhaps your wife or girlfriend's parents. Use this bow in any situation when you need to show someone a moderate amount of respect.

Start this bow by standing in the seiritsu position and bend your upper body forward at a 45-degree angle. This bend forward will happen over the span of one breath. Inhale as you move into the bow and exhale when your body is at the correct angle. Move your hands down the front of your legs at the same time and at the same speed as you move your upper body. Your hands should stop just above your knees, about 7 to 10 cm. When you return to the standing position, do it over the span of a slow inhalation.

There are three more important bows used in Japanese culture, but I see no reason for a tourist to learn these bows.

The saikeirei bow, or the "deeply reverent" bow is used to show profound regret or respect. This bow is also used in religious situations. The saikeirei bow can be performed in both a standing and sitting position. This bow is considered to be a dramatic bow and there will be little to no instances when you need to use this bow as a tourist.

Nirei-Nihakushu is known as the "Worship" bow. This will usually be performed while visiting a Shinto shrine. It is more of a specific ritual and it combines 2 keirei bows with one saikeirei bow, along with some claps. Although not required, you may want to perform this bow if you visit any Shinto shrine during your visit to Japan. If you do, then this bow will be provided in the "Visiting Shrines" section of this book.

The dogeza bow is known as the "begging for your life" bow. This bow is essentially groveling and begging someone for their mercy. You may have seen someone do this in a samurai movie when they have done something extremely disrespectful. This bow is done by someone who is feeling great shame or fear for their life. You do not need to know this bow as there will be no situation in which you need to use it. Most Japanese people barely have any use for this bow themselves.

Rule of Thumb:

All of these different types of bows can be confusing and frustrating. Even after you take the time to learn them all, you may find yourself forgetting certain things and messing up. If this is the case, there are some simple things to remember when you are in doubt of what to do in any situation. Keep these things in mind if you are unsure about when or how to bow.

1. Bow to someone when they bow to you. This will exclude certain people such as clerks in a shop or people handing out things on the street. However, this should work in any situation. If someone bows to you just bow back.

2. If you are unsure as to which bow to use in which situation, then just bow to about a 30-degree angle. This is an acceptable bow in almost all situations as it shows a moderate amount of respect and a good balance of familiarity. This can be done in both sitting and standing positions.

3. If you don't know how long or deep to bow to someone, then use age and titles as a determining factor. You can probably get away with guessing someone's age. The older they are then the deeper and longer

you hold a bow for. The deeper and longer the bow, the more respect you are showing. If you are unsure of someone's title, then just get a hold of their business or name card. The Japanese are very willing to hand out their cards.

4. Some places might have a specific way they want people to bow. If you are working in a company that prefers a certain type of bow, then just follow their instructions. Look to your coworkers for guidance.

5. If you are still unsure about the length of your bow, then simply hold your bow a second longer than the person you are bowing to. If you are in a group, then look to the person who is the closest to your rank and bow just a second longer than them.

6. When you bow you bow from the waist. Don't curve your neck or your spine. Keep them both as straight as they were when you were standing up. A curved back during a bow is bad form and improper etiquette.

Don'ts of Bowing:

There are certain things that you can get away with doing if you are a tourist. However, there are also certain things that you should try to avoid doing no matter what.

1. Don't place your palms together and keep your hands in front of your chest while bowing. This is the original Chinese Buddhism way to bow, but it is not done in Japan anymore. You will mostly keep your hands by your sides or on your legs in front of you.

2. Don't bow while walking. Always stop moving then bow before you continue walking.

3. Bowing while on a chair is sometimes too informal for some situations. If the person that is bowing to you is standing, then it's better to stand up and bow to them.

4. Never bow while speaking. This is rude and disrespectful. Rather say what you need to say before you bow or wait till after you bow to speak. In some cases, mostly when apologizing, it is okay to bow and apologize

at the same time. However, with some people who prefer to stick to the rules, if you bow and apologize at the same time, you may anger them more. Rather be cautious in this instance and apologize before or after your bow.

5. If you are in a situation when you need to bow to someone on a set of stairs, never bow when you are a stair above them. Wait until they are on the same stair as you or move down onto their stair before you bow. You must always be on the same level as someone when you are bowing.

6. If it is visibly clear that you are angry or upset then do not bow to someone. Bowing is used to show respect and every part of your body needs to show that when you are bowing. If you are angry, upset, or frustrated then do not bow.

7. Some men place their hands on the sides of their behinds while bowing, but this is incorrect. Sometimes a certain company will prefer you bow this way but if not then don't do it. Men should place their hands on the front of their thighs.

8. Sometimes, women will put their hands together, either side by side or on top of each other, and let their hands hang in front of their legs while bowing. This is not the traditional way for women to bow. However, it has become a popular way for women to bow among the younger generation. It is seen as being more feminine and delicate. This is not an incorrect way to bow, but keep in mind that it is not the traditional way to bow either.

9. Don't bow and shake hands at the same time. Sometimes, a tourist, especially in business situations, will shake someone's hand and bow to them simultaneously. This is awkward and looks silly. Don't do it. Either shake someone's hand or bow to them, not both at the same time.

As you can see, bowing is a form of art and lifestyle in Japan. There are so many dos and don'ts to remember while bowing. If you want to keep things simple remember that most Japanese will let you get away with a few simple mistakes as they don't even expect you to bow in the first place. However, if you want to experience the fullness of Japan and all it has to offer then dedicate a few moments of your day to learning about and practicing bowing.

How to Shake Hands

Shaking hands is not a very common thing in Japan as it is more of a Western custom. Throughout most of Japan's history, the bow has been the widely accepted form of greeting. However, in modern times, the Western handshake is becoming more widely accepted, but it has come nowhere near replacing the importance of the traditional bow. The handshake has shown up in most segments in their society, but you'll find that a bow will take precedence over a handshake in most situations.

The main reason for the rise in the new custom is because of the rise in tourism. The Japanese do not expect visitors from other countries to know or even care about their customs. They will hardly ever expect a tourist to bow in any situation that requires one, so they started accepting handshakes instead. Nowadays, virtually all Japanese people, including women, will accept a handshake from a foreigner almost automatically. Some will accept a handshake and still offer up a bow because it is still their way. Although it is not required of you to bow in any given situation, you will be more welcomed and accepted if you do show respect for their culture and customs.

In any case, you'll probably only see a handshake being used in the world of business rather than in any formal or informal event or occasion. Still, it is best to know the dos and don'ts of a Japanese handshake just in case you need to use one during your visit.

Some Japanese use a combination of both a bow and a handshake during greetings and introductions, while other Japanese, especially of the older generation, prefer only a bow that fits their social status. In cases where a combination of a handshake and a bow are used, remember that the bow will take precedence over the handshake. This means that you should bow first and then proceed to offer a handshake. Also, during large events or meetings, it may not be practical to bow and shake everyone's hand individually. In this case, it's best to skip the handshake and simply bow.

If you're going to be shaking hands during your visit to Japan, it is best to learn to shake hands the Japanese way first. In Western tradition, a handshake should come with a firm grip and a strong shake to show that you are a strong and trustworthy person, and it can also be a sign of a friendly and positive attitude. However, in Japan, a firm grip and a strong shake may come across the wrong way. It will be seen as a threatening action if you shake someone's hand and your grip is firmer than theirs. The Japanese usually offer a relatively weak handshake and it is in your best interest to try and match that while shaking someone's hand. This is probably because the handshake is not indigenous to their culture and some Japanese, especially of the older generation, are still uncomfortable with it.

The way to shake hands in Japan can be simple if you remember to follow a few simple rules. Wait for them to offer you their hand. This is because some Japanese may still prefer a bow over a handshake and will not want one unless you offer it yourself. Make sure they offer up their hand first, and then you'll know it is okay. When you take their hand try and gauge the strength of their grip as soon as possible. Once you've done this, match their grip if possible. You don't want to have higher grip strength than them; either have it be the same or lower. Don't let the handshake last for too long. A few brief seconds will be enough.

If you want to show some extra respect or politeness, you can give them a bow once the handshake is over. If you are in a business situation and you want to give them your name card, then you can do this the traditional way instead of just giving them a bow.

During your first meeting with someone, you can try and read them beforehand. Sometimes you will be able to tell what someone expects from you by the way they hold themselves. If you see someone reaching for a name card, then that's a cue for you to follow suit. If they are extending their hand out for a handshake then by all means take it. A person's body language can make it easier for you to understand what they expect from you as long as you are watching closely enough. As a rule of thumb, the older generation will be more traditional than the younger generation. If you're dealing with an older person, then it's best to stick to tradition as much as possible.

Chapter 3

The Importance of the Group

The Japanese are very group-orientated as their culture (and many other non-Western cultures) is collectivist rather than individualist. Their groups extend further than just their family. Every part of their lives is centered on being a member in a group. It's important for them to be in some kind of group because to be without a group in their culture is the equivalent of not existing.

The need to meld with others is socially important and it has been for a very long time. It's not just important socially; being a part of a group is also essential for their survival. A popular Japanese proverb can maybe help explain the importance of the group in Japan, it goes: "The head of the nail that sticks up is pounded down." This means, basically, that if you are different or if you stick out then you will be forced to conform.

The threat of being ostracized or left out is one of the most devastating thoughts to the Japanese. The fundamental concept for understanding the group ethnic in Japan is the phrase amae, pronounced ah-mah-ee. It means "to look to others for affection" and can help explain the deep need the Japanese have to be part of a group.

From a young age, as early as possible, Japanese children are taught to be loyal to each other and to depend on and take responsibility for the group they are in. The Japanese grow up learning to place the desires and needs of the group ahead of their own needs and desires. This was critical for their survival outside of their family. They needed to establish themselves in a group in their school and other parts of their social life; otherwise they would be left out and essentially become invisible.

There are even social rankings within a group. There is the inside circle, those who are in it are the closest in the group and are basically like family. These members are part of the group for life and virtually nothing can break the bond between them. Then there is the outside circle. Those within this circle are still part of the group, but they are not as close to any of the members and are capable of losing their spot in the group if they do something worthy of that. Then you get everyone else who is outside of the group completely, these people are practically no one to those within the group.

You'll find that most Japanese will be part of multiple groups, but no two groups will ever come together. Each group is separate and each group plays an important role in their life. Each group is also the equivalent of an extended family. The groups are a part of their lives that can't be replaced or removed without causing some serious damage.

The modern concept of amae is related to the concept of wa (harmony.) This is the way that harmony has managed to survive throughout history. The importance of the group extends to the importance of harmony. Without the group ethic, there would be little harmony. Everyone sticks to their group and becomes one with others. They look for guidance and gratification from their group. The group ethic can be seen in every part of Japan - in schools, in the workplace, and in other social areas of life. There are still a few instances when individualism is encouraged over a group. Hobbies like art, music, and gardening are seen as individual areas and there is no need for you to be a part of a group while doing it.

Understanding the importance of the group in Japan will help you greatly when it comes to forming relationships and introducing yourself to people while you're there.

'Cold' Introductions

Due to Japan being so deeply group-orientated, introducing yourself to someone new is an extremely difficult task. Self-introductions are so frowned upon that they are widely known as 'cold' introductions. They are considered to be impolite and untraditional for a few reasons. One, in order to introduce yourself, you had to be somewhat of an aggressive person. Shy and unaggressive people are far less likely to introduce themselves, so if you did introduce yourself you were seen as aggressive and this would risk angering someone. Two, a group was always reluctant to take on any new members as they were seen as obligations and it wasn't in the group's best interest if they didn't know you. Three, there is no way for the group to prove your claims or verify who you are. Four, there was no mutual friend or party there to prove your claims, vouch for you, or take responsibility for you if you do enter the group.

Every stranger that was outside the group was kept at a safe distance. Since everyone is in a group in Japan that means it is very difficult for any newcomers to be welcomed. This did not mean that those inside the group were impolite to those outside of the group. They remained polite to everyone. However, their politeness was a way of keeping strangers at a safe distance. It was a kind of politeness that would push someone away rather than welcome them in. Someone was only able to get into a group if they were introduced to the group by a trusted third party or someone that was already in the group. This is why someone wouldn't introduce themselves. It was better for them to be introduced to the group by someone else.

As a tourist and a visitor to Japan, you probably won't have to worry about the group ethic or 'cold' introduction too much. Since globalization, the Japanese have become very open to tourists and visitors. Many of them are more than happy to meet you and be your friend. Since self-introductions are not common in Japan, it would be best to perform a proper introduction and leave nothing to chance.

When meeting someone new it's always best to start with a 'hello' or 'konnichiwa.' If it's during the night, then you can say 'good evening' or 'konbanwa. Then you can say 'nice to meet you' or hajimemashite.

Whether you want to perform your self-introduction in English or Japanese is up to you, but being able to speak a little Japanese will show that you respect their culture and will earn you a few points.

After opening up the conversation with any of the above options you can follow with your name. "My name is…your name…" or you can say in Japanese "…your name…to iimasu," and if you want someone to call you by a nickname or shortened version of your name you can say, "please call me…your nickname…" or "…your nickname…to yonde kudasai."

Now you can tell everybody what your nationality is and where you're from. You can also maybe say what your job is or state a few of your hobbies and strengths. You want to make it easier for someone to get to know you, but you don't want it to look like you're showing off. People will want to know what you enjoy and what your strengths are, but they won't appreciate you coming across too proud. Try and be humble during this part. Too much information will come across as bragging and you can spoil the relationship from the start.

When you are done saying everything you want to say, it's a good idea to end off your introduction with a bow. This doesn't have to be a bow showing too much respect but it should be more than just a head nod. You want to show the person that you are polite and you respect them as your equal. A quick, 30-degree bow will do. If this person is of a higher social ranking than you, like your boss, then a deeper and longer bow is required to show more respect.

This is a lot to remember and it seems like a complicated way to introduce yourself but don't take it too seriously. Remember that the Japanese, especially of the younger generation, are eager to meet tourists. You'll be welcomed with open arms even if you don't want to be. People will ask you a lot of questions and you should just do your best to answer them. When in doubt, it never hurts to be nice, so just smile, nod, be nice, and you'll be perfectly fine.

Chapter 4

Going Out

When we are in the comfort of our own homes, we aren't obligated to do anything and we can behave how we want. Some people even walk around in their underwear because they feel free when they do, and that's okay. When you're in your own home, you set the rules. You can dictate what is right and wrong behavior. However, when you go out in public, all of that changes. There are rules you need to follow in order to conform to society. There are standards you're expected to meet so you aren't treated like an outsider by the people around you. You wouldn't walk around in public without your pants on.

This is true for any country, and especially Japan. In Japan, there is an etiquette for almost every situation. Going to a restaurant, drinking with friends or coworkers, eating, paying the bill, and even sitting has a certain etiquette and protocol that needs to be followed. Public situations can be nerve-racking and complicated. This simple guide will help you to know exactly what you can and can't do when going out in Japan.

Seating

As stated before, Japanese society was originally arranged in a vertical way. The social system took this vertical form with the highest-ranking members, like the emperor, at the top and the lowest ranking members, like merchants and farmers, at the bottom. The exact same vertical formation can be seen in the Japanese seating protocol.

It seems silly that everyone would have a certain place they are allowed to sit, but this kind of thinking was crucial to their social system back then. You will see this kind of seating protocol in Western society as well. It's the same as when the father of a house sits at the head of a table, or the owner of business sits at the head of the table during a meeting. The father and the owner are essentially the highest-ranking people in those situations. They are seated at the head of the table because they are higher in the social system than the others in the room. This can also be seen at parties when the children sit at a children's table separate from the adults. The children are ranked lower than the adults, so they sit at a table designated for them which is of lower standard than the adult's table. You see it at a wedding where the bride, groom and close members of the family sit at the head of the room. Then everyone around them is arranged from closest family and friends, or the most important people, to the least important people at the back. These situations and others make up the vertical society that we often don't even notice. It is no different in Japan.

The vertical society was abolished in Japan a long time ago, but that didn't stop everyone who grew up living a certain way to continue to live that way. Centuries of following the system don't just end when someone says that it does. Needless to say, this means that the old seating protocol is still very alive and used in Japan.

Following the seating protocol in Japan won't be as difficult as you may think. The seating protocol is very similar to that of Western society and the vertical social system. The highest-ranking people or seniors are placed at the head or the top while those ranking lower are placed in order below. This is true for any situation involving more than two people. It's the same not just for sitting situations but also for standing situations, like for a photo.

Usually the highest-ranking member of the group or the guest of honor at a gathering would take the kami-za, which means the seat of honor and is pronounced kah-me-zah. The seat of honor is the highest seat at the table. If it is someone's birthday and you are going out to dinner, they would most likely be given the seat of honor. If you are going to a dinner party, the host will most likely receive the seat of honor unless they offer it to someone they see as being a higher rank than them.

Try to avoid any confusion as to which seat is the seat of honor. You don't want to accidentally sit in it. In any room or situation, the seat of honor is usually the farthest away from the entrance and at the head of the table or room. If there is a room that has windows only on one side, then that side is usually designated as the head of the room. The seat of honor should always be facing the entrance. The same as if you enter someone's office where their desk is facing the door and there are windows behind them. This is essentially the seat of honor.

In any informal or semiformal situation, a group of Japanese people will usually sort themselves out when it comes to seating order. They will know who among them the highest-ranking is and who is the lowest and arrange themselves accordingly. In more formal situations, the seats will probably be chosen for each person ahead of time by whoever is arranging the gathering. This can be seen by place markers or name cards on the table.

As a foreigner, you may not have to worry about where to sit in any situation. If you are invited to a formal gathering of any kind, the hosts will most likely show you to your seat. If you are invited to an informal or semiformal situation of any kind, one Japanese member of the group will take it upon themselves to show you where you should sit. As the visitor to their country, your host may want to make you feel comfortable and want to impress you. This means that you might even be seated next to the seat of honor on most occasions. If you are unsure as to where to sit, just wait until someone comes and shows you where to go. This is the safest action for you to take.

If you are hosting a gathering and you are inviting Japanese people, then it is usually up to you to determine where everyone sits. You may want to seat yourself in the seat of honor. This is an option given to you as you are the host. However, to show extra politeness and gratitude it is important that you direct one of your Japanese guests of the highest rank towards the seat of honor. They may try to refuse but you should insist. If they do show reluctance, just keep insisting they take the seat, in a friendly and playful manner, and eventually they will accept. This is the humble and right thing to do. You will be revered for it by your Japanese guests and it will earn you some brownie points.

On a side note, if you're eating in a casual setting, say a coffee shop or a fast-food restaurant, you are allowed to save your seat. In Western society, it is often seen as selfish to save a seat for yourself. In other words, you walk into a coffee shop, place a personal object on the seat you want to take, and then leave to use the bathroom or do something in your car quickly even before you order so that no one else can take your seat. This is usually frowned upon in Western society. However, you are perfectly okay to do this in Japan as long as it is in a casual setting and not a formal dining area.

It's important to note that there are even seating and standing protocols in things like the elevator, in a car, on a train, when walking as a group, and in an airplane. You may not have to worry about these things, but just in case, you should know where the place of honor is in each situation. The place of honor in an elevator is in the center, closest to the back wall. The place of honor in a car is the backseat, directly behind the driver of the car. The place of honor in a train is the center seat or window seat. The place of honor while walking in a group is directly in the center of the group. The place of honor on an airplane is usually a window seat around the middle of the cabin and on the right side which is away from the door. As long as you avoid the place of honor in any situation, you should be fine to sit or stand anywhere else you want.

Dining and Eating

Dining and eating out in Japan can be a minefield of etiquette. There are so many dos and don'ts that it is easy to make a mistake if you aren't careful. As a visitor to the country, no one expects you to know the proper way to do things. This means that you will probably be forgiven if you make a mistake as long as it isn't too big. However, knowing all the rights and wrongs is a part of the whole experience. If you're anything like me, you'll want to make a good impression, and the best way to do that is to study and practice the proper dining and eating etiquette in Japan.

The rules that come with eating out and dining in Japan are basically just widely desired and accepted manners. Every society and culture in the world has these kinds of manners. You wouldn't want someone chewing with their mouth open or talking while their mouth is full during dinner. This is dining and eating etiquette. If you look at it this way, you'll see that we aren't that different from the Japanese, we all have our rules to follow. Let's take a look at what rules you'll have to follow when eating and dining in Japan.

Sitting:

You already know about the seating protocol in Japan, but there is also a certain way to sit. In some dining areas, you'll be expected to sit in the traditional Japanese fashion. There will be low to the floor dining tables and cushions placed on a tatami floor, which is a reed mat. You've probably seen these kinds of situations in a movie or two.

In a formal situation, both men and women will be expected to sit in a kneeling position, like the seated bow seiza. You will get into the kneeling position the same way. Men kneel down one knee at a time and women kneel down with both knees at once. It is important to practice sitting in this position as it can be quite straining over long periods of time, so you need to build up the flexibility and tolerance beforehand.

In an informal situation, men will be allowed to sit cross-legged and women can sit with both legs to one side. Women should never sit cross-legged even if they are not wearing a dress.

Washing Your Hands:

In most bars and restaurants in Japan, you will be given a steamed, hot towel before your meal. This towel is used to clean your hands. Do not use the towel for any purpose other than to clean your hands. It is considered rude to use the towel to wipe your face or anything else. The towel will be removed when you are finished with it.

If you are eating at home or at someone else's home, you should go to the bathroom and wash your hands before you sit down to eat.

Starting a Meal:

A meal will usually begin when the main guest, host, head family member, or the waitress makes a gesture. This gesture will show that it is okay to start eating. This gesture may be the use of the term itadakimasu. This means "I gratefully receive." This is a form of gratitude and it may be used to start a meal.

When you are about to sit down and eat, you should wait until the most important person at the table has seated. When they have started eating, then it is okay for you to start. If you are the host or honored guest, then you can wait until everyone else has seated before you start the meal.

Chopstick Etiquette:

There are a lot of rules when it comes to the use of chopsticks. Chopsticks are the main object during any eating or dining situation and it's important that you learn to use them correctly.

Chopsticks should be held properly and used properly. To hold your chopsticks, think of the way you would hold a pen or pencil. Hold the one chopstick this way. Then, slide the second chopstick in between the tips of your index finger and thumb. Now you should be holding the top chopstick loosely with your index finger and thumb and the bottom chopstick with the rest of your fingers, the same way you would hold a pen or pencil. To use the chopsticks, simply lift your thumb and index finger slightly. This will lift the top chopstick but keep the bottom one in place. To grab a piece of food, lower your index finger and thumb. This will lower the top chopstick down onto the bottom chopstick and grab the piece of food. It's important to practice this as eating with chopsticks can be challenging and straining on the fingers.

Do not stab your food with the chopsticks the same way you would with a fork. This is rude and unacceptable. Also, you should always be able to eat your food in one bite. If you pick something up to eat, don't bite part of it off and put the rest back. You should be able to fit the whole piece in your mouth, if not then try to break it up in the bowl before you pick it up. On a side note, you should never lift your food higher than your mouth.

Don't leave your chopsticks inside your bowl when you aren't using them. This is similar to an offering shown at funerals so don't do it in a normal dining situation. When you are finished eating your meal or you aren't using your chopsticks, place them on a hashioki or a chopstick stand. In the absence of a chopstick stand, you can place your chopsticks over the top of your bowl or neatly at the edge of your plate.

Don't speak while holding your chopsticks. If you want to have a chat with someone, put your chopsticks down and wait till the conversation is over before picking them back up. Also, don't point or gesture using your chopsticks. They are eating utensils and should be used only for eating.

Sometimes there will be a communal plate of food in the center of the table. This food is for the table to share. Do not eat directly from this plate. Use your chopsticks to take something from this plate and place it on your own. Don't pick up the food from the plate and put it directly in your mouth. After you have placed it on your plate, wait a moment before eating it. Also, you should never pass someone food using your chopsticks to someone else's chopsticks. It is rude to exchange food from one set of chopsticks to another. Either lift a plate up for them to pick from or place the food in a plate that they are holding. To be on the safe side, try to avoid passing anyone food at all.

If you feel you are unable to use chopsticks properly, you could always ask the host or waitress if they have a knife and fork for you to use. You're a foreigner so they won't be angry if you can't use chopsticks. In fact, someone may even be happy to help you and show you how to use them. A restaurant will probably have a knife and fork for you to use, but if you're at someone's house, they may not. If they don't, then it's fine. By asking them for a knife and fork, you have let them know that you are unsure how to use chopsticks so any mistake you make will be forgiven.

Holding Your Bowl:

When eating from a small bowl, it is actually considered good manners to raise your bowl close to your mouth. You should pick your bowl up with one hand cupped over the bottom and lift it up near your mouth. Only do this when you are eating from it. If you are done eating or taking a break, place the bowl back down. You should do this to avoid dropping any food. It's rude to cup your hand underneath your mouth to catch food while eating; it is better to lift the bowl up so you can catch food that may drop.

Drinking During a Meal:

When drinking in Japan, it is customary to wait until the whole table raises their glasses in cheers before drinking any alcohol. If you want to drink alcohol while eating, then you will have to wait for these moments before drinking. However, you are allowed to sip on water or a soda while eating your food. Keep this in mind and make sure to order a glass of water or soda along with your alcoholic drink.

Ordering Food:

Ordering food while in a restaurant is actually pretty simple. If you are ordering just one thing for yourself, then all you need to do is say the name of the item you want to eat and add a "please" at the end. This is if you are dining out by yourself and just want to eat one item. If you are dining out with friends and coworkers, it's likely you won't all be ordering one item each. In most of these situations, communal plates will be ordered for the table so everyone can share the same food. If this is true, then you don't have to worry about ordering at all. Usually the host or honored person will be the one ordering for the whole table. You just need to eat what they order.

Eating:

There are certain ways to eat certain types of food in Japan. Sushi is eaten using your hands just as much as using chopsticks nowadays in Japan. It is perfectly okay for you to pick up your sushi with your hands as well as with your chopsticks. Sushi is usually eaten with wasabi and soy sauce. You'll be given a separate shallow bowl for your soy sauce. Pour the amount of sauce you think you'll be using into the bowl and dip your sushi into it. Try to be delicate when dipping the sushi as you don't want any part of the sushi breaking up into the sauce. You can put the wasabi on top of your sushi using chopsticks but don't mix the wasabi into the soy sauce. This is seen as being an insult to the chef. Make sure to leave a little bit of soy sauce in the shallow bowl when you are done. It shouldn't be left empty.

Soup in Japan is usually quite different from soup in other countries. It usually contains lots of solid ingredients, so spoons are not needed. You can and are expected to eat soup with chopsticks. When eating miso soup, you can drink the liquid from the bowl as if it were a cup and then pick up the solids using a chopstick. Don't be afraid to slurp your noodles in noodle soup. In Japan, it is good to slurp your soup because they believe that inhaling air while eating noodles can improve its taste. Do not finish your soup before eating the rest of your meal because your soup should accompany the rest of the meal. Make sure to replace the lid of the soup bowl when you are finished.

Clams are not often eaten in Japan, but when they are, there are rules to eating them. You can eat them with your hands or with chopsticks. If the clams come in a bowl with soup, then it is better to use your chopsticks. Do not leave the empty clam shells on a separate plate or anything. This is rude. The clam shells should be left in the bowl they came in.

Empty Plate or Cup:

An empty plate, bowl, or cup is seen as a desire to eat or drink more. If you are truly finished eating and you don't want to eat anymore, leave a little bit of food on your plate. It's the same if you don't want to drink anymore. If you are finished with your meal and have emptied your plate, just take a bit more food from a communal plate and put it in yours. Make sure to return your chopsticks to their stand when you're done.

Sampling Everything:

Usually, communal dishes are placed along the middle of the table and everyone can take what they want. You don't have to eat a lot of food, but it is polite to at least sample everything that's on the table. Try eating one of everything if it's possible.

If you are offered food, it is polite to hesitate slightly before accepting it. Don't just instantly agree to take the food you're offered. It's seen as rude or greedy to be so eager to accept food. It's also seen as rude to deny it. The safest thing to do is hesitate slightly and then accept it.

Tipping Waiters or Waitresses:

In some cultures, it is seen as cheap and rude if you do not tip a waiter or waitress, especially if they have done a good job. In Japan, it is the opposite. It's advised that you don't tip the person serving you as it can be seen as rude and demeaning to them. Often, waiters and waitresses train very hard for a long time to become good at their job. In Japan, they take great pride in anything they do, so you can see why they would see a tip as demeaning and rude. Don't feel the need to tip them because they did a good job. The fact that they did a good job and your thank you at the end of the meal is rewarding enough for them.

Ending a Meal:

When you are ending a meal, make sure to return the table back to the way you found it. Place your chopsticks back on their stand or back into the paper holder they came in. Replace any lids back on to the bowls they were removed from. Make sure the table is clean and neat.

To show gratitude and thanks for the meal, you can say, "gochisosama deshita", this means "thank you for the meal." Give a slight bow of the head to your host, the waitress, or the chef if they are present, while saying this.

If all this information feels overwhelming, do not worry too much since these rules are seen more as social guidelines. Some of the rules above are seen as being very important, but some of them aren't as important. As always, remember that you are a visitor to their country and most Japanese people will not expect you to know everything about their country or their customs. They will be more than happy to help you learn if they see that you don't know how to do something. Any mistakes you make will be forgiven as long as you're willing to learn from those mistakes and try not to do it again.

Drinking in Japan

Drinking in Japan is a big thing for both social and business situations. There is always a reason to drink in Japan, but, just like everything else, there is a certain etiquette to follow when you go out drinking. There are a lot of dos and don'ts of drinking, but perhaps one of the most important things to know is how to say "cheers!" I know it doesn't sound appealing to have to follow rules when all you want to do is drink, but it's actually simpler than it seems.

Cheers!

Being able to say "cheers" in Japan is more important to drinking than you may think. It is the most important part of drinking. If no one says "cheers" then it's likely that no one will drink. There are several ways to say cheers in Japan, but the simplest and most common word used is "kanpai", which is pronounced gahn-pie. The word kanpai is usually yelled out with a great deal of enthusiasm and everyone raises their glasses at the sound of this word. The word basically means "empty glasses" and is the equivalent to the western phrase "bottoms up."

Traditionally, people were expected to finish their drinks, which were usually sake, pronounced sah-keh or rice wine, in one sip. This is why the cups they drink out of are the size of shot glasses or smaller. Sake is a very strong drink. Drinking too much of it will get you drunk very quickly, even with the small glasses. Beer is becoming a commonly ordered drink now in Japan, but don't worry, you won't have to chug the whole glass down every time some yells kanpai. Whenever someone offers a toast you can simply take a sip of your drink.

Kanpai is the most used form of cheers in Japan and can be used in almost all informal social events. There are other forms of saying cheers though. "Omedetou", pronounced oh-meh-deh-toe, is a toast that means "congratulations" in Japanese and is used in such events.

There will be lots of cheering throughout the night and at some point, someone will yell out, "banzai". This means "to live 10,000 years," and when it is called out, everyone raises their glasses and brings them together before all drinking. Try and be as enthusiastic as possible during this part. You don't want to be the only one there who doesn't seem excited about living for 10,000 years.

That's the basics of saying cheers while drinking in Japan. Remember that anyone can say cheers if they want to, even you.

Meet and Greet:

Unless you are already acquainted with everyone at the table, take some time to introduce yourself politely. Make an effort to meet everyone that is going to be out and drinking that night. You might go out with people you know, but then they could invite someone who invites someone else. These people will be strangers to you. Don't treat them as such, make an effort to be polite and introduce yourself the traditional way. Remember to smile and bow or shake hands when it is appropriate.

Never Drink Alone:

You already know that the Japanese are group orientated. The same rules apply to drinking. You should try to avoid drinking alone as it isn't the Japanese way, besides, there will probably always be someone that will come have a drink with you if you ask. That is one of the first things you will learn about drinking in Japan.

Don't go out drinking alone and don't take a drink from your glass alone. Wait until the whole group has received their drink before you even think about touching yours. Before you can take a sip from your drink, someone has to say kanpai. If you want to drink, then feel free to say it yourself. If not, then you can wait for someone else to say it. When someone says kanpai, raise your glass, make eye contact with those nearest to you and pay attention to the one who is giving the toast. You don't have to touch glasses unless someone else initiates it. Whether you are touching glasses or not, make sure your glass is below that of someone of higher social ranking than you. This is especially important in a business outing. You can take a sip or down your shot when everyone else does. You never drink alone as it is seen as rude.

Holding Your Cup:

During a toast, you should hold your cup a certain way. When you lift your cup up, especially if it is a sake cup, women should always put their hand underneath the cup. Women should hold the cup from the bottom and men should do this when toasting to someone of a higher rank than them. This is a sign of respect.

The First Drink:

This isn't a requirement, but it's good form, polite, and good for the group if your first drink is the same as everyone else's. Drinking in Japan is all about sharing an experience, either with your coworkers or your friends. After the first drink, you can order any drink you want. However, it's better if you order with the group at first. Japan is very big on team players. You can show them just how much of a team player you are by sacrificing your first drink so you can order with the group. Remember you have a whole night of drinking ahead of you so you can have whatever you want afterwards.

When it comes to ordering the first drink, don't try to be the one that does it, unless you know for certain what everyone is going to like. It's safer to just agree with whatever everyone else wants to get. Usually, the person with the highest social ranking will be the deciding factor. That's okay. You'll earn yourself a lot of points if you agree with their choice.

What Should You Drink?

Sake is a traditional and still a very popular drink in Japan. However, if you order this, you usually order for the whole table as it comes in a sharing bottle and not a glass for one person. Beer has gained some traction in Japan and so has bourbon and whiskey. These are popular choices in Japan. If you are out with friends or coworkers, they may want to drink sake with you. It's better if you drink with them rather than turn them down. Sake has been and still is an important part of the Japanese culture since the 8th century so it isn't a good idea to turn them down if they offer it to you.

Pouring Drinks:

When drinking in Japan, you should never pour your own drink or let someone else pour their own drink. If your glass is empty, someone sitting near you will offer to fill it. They will probably fill it from a bottle that they are drinking from or from a bottle that the whole table is sharing. They will of course offer to fill your glass before they pour, and it is better for you to accept their offer rather than turn it down.

While they are pouring your drink, hold your glass with both hands and pay attention. It is rude to be looking at your phone or talking to someone else while someone is pouring your drink. When they are done pouring, thank them with a smile and a bow of your head to be polite.

During the evening, you will be expected to reciprocate. If someone who is seated near you has an empty glass, then offer to fill it for them. Offer to fill it either using the bottle the table is sharing, the bottle you are drinking from, or the bottle they are drinking from. If you are drinking the same thing then it is okay to fill their glass using the bottle you're drinking from. It's rude to try and change what someone is drinking. Always offer before you pour. If they accept, then pour carefully and try not to spill anything. Cleanliness is very appreciated in Japan. By the end of the night it would be ideal if you have offered to refill everyone's glass, but don't worry about this. Don't rush to refill someone's drink; if the opportunity arises you can take it but don't hold your breath for it. You should always reciprocate if someone pours a drink for you.

Traditionally, those of lower social status or who are younger will pour drinks for the higher ranking or older members of the group. Someone may refuse to let you pour their drink a couple of times. If they do, then it may not be because they are done drinking, but it may be because they are exercising humility. This is a valued trait to have in Japan.

If you want to refuse when someone asks to refill your cup, you don't need to shake your head or say no to them, as this can come across rude or aggressive. Simply place your hand over your cup and smile at them. This is the most polite way of saying no to having your drink refilled.

Pouring:

When pouring someone's drink, remember that the hand pouring should always be pouring forward. Never pour backwards or at an angle.

Done Drinking:

When you have reached your limit and can't drink anymore, don't feel ashamed or get worried. When you're done drinking, you can simply stop. No one will shame you for it because it will be against etiquette to embarrass someone because of their lack of tolerance. They either won't say anything or they will understand and leave you alone.

To stop drinking you can leave your glass full. An empty glass usually indicates that you aren't finished drinking. If someone sees that your glass is empty, they will offer to fill it. If you don't want this to happen, you can simply leave your glass full.

You can still participate when someone says kanpai and lift your glass. You can even fake a small sip of your glass. Eventually, they will get that you are done drinking or they won't even notice.

Drinking While Eating:

If you're drinking in a group during a meal make sure you remember the drinking alone rule. You may want to take a sip of your drink in between bites but you should avoid this. If you are feeling thirsty then you can drink some water rather than take a sip of your alcohol. It is appropriate to drink alcohol only when someone says kanpai and everyone raises their glasses.

If you do want a sip of your drink but don't want to wait for a kanpai or cause one yourself, there is a way around it. You can simply raise your glass and meet eyes with someone. They will see the gesture and raise their glass and you can both take a drink together. During the meal, someone may make eye contact with you and expect the same thing. If this happens, don't hesitate or ignore the gesture. Raise your glass up the moment you see the gesture, keep eye contact with them, and take a drink.

Ending the Night:

If you are leaving or if someone else is leaving the expression, "otsukaresama deshita", which means "you're tired," is often used. This is a way of telling someone that they have done a good job and have worked hard. It is a nice way of telling a friend or associate that they are tired because they are a good worker. They have given all they can and are deserving of some rest.

When you are tired and ready to leave, prepare to hear these words. Remember to be polite and say your goodbyes. Perhaps offer a single bow to the group as you leave and thank them for a good night. Keep in mind that no one will shame you if you feel that you are leaving too early. Everyone has their tolerance levels and you will not be shamed for yours.

Paying the Bill:

This is probably one of the simplest things to learn about dining in Japan. The bill is usually paid by the host or the honored guest. Generally speaking, whoever invited everyone out to eat is the person that should be paying the bill for the night. It is rude to offer or insist to pay for yourself unless it was previously agreed that everyone would be splitting the bill. Keep this in mind when you are inviting people out to eat or drink with you that you may be expected to pay the bill for the night.

The most important thing to remember about drinking in Japan is that it is seen as a group activity. If you go out drinking with others, you are expected to be a team player. It is not about the individual. The group is supposed to be enjoying the experience together. They share it all, including hangovers!

Public Etiquette

If you're in Japan for the first time, it may not be easy to notice all of the subtle ways that people act and hold themselves in public. You may be forgiven for not knowing certain Japanese customs because you're a tourist, but you don't want to be an annoying tourist, do you? You'd be surprised what things you can do in public that will be seen as rude or annoying to the Japanese. The easiest way to avoid doing these things is by knowing what they are.

No Eating, Drinking, or Smoking While Walking:

Japan is big on showing consideration for the people around you. While in some places it is convenient and okay to walk around eating your lunch or smoking, it's considered rude in Japan. This attitude comes from your habits inconveniencing those around you.

If you're walking around eating or drinking something while you're walking through the streets, then you may spill or drop some food on the ground. Someone could end up stepping in this later on and then their day will be ruined. It's also not nice to litter or make a mess on the streets. Someone has to clean it up.

The same approach is taken with smoking. You shouldn't walk around in public while smoking a cigarette because you'll be blowing smoke all over other people walking near you. These people could be against smoking or they may not want you smoking anywhere near their children.

There are designated outdoor smoking areas where it is okay for you to stand still and smoke. Most convenience stores will also have a seating area outside so you can sit down and eat or drink your food instead of walking around.

Don't Count Change:

In most tourist destinations and other countries, you will feel obligated to count the change given to you at any store. In Japan, you must resist the urge to do so. It is seen as rude to count the change that is handed to you. It shows that you do not trust the person giving it to you. Be assured that Japan is not like all the other tourist places around the world. Your change will be correct. Whatever you do, don't count it.

Don't Blow Your Nose:

In Western culture, they prefer that you blow your nose instead of sniffing all the time. However, in Japan, it is the opposite. Blowing your nose in public, especially loudly, is seen as being extremely rude in Japan. It's better to turn away from a crowd and discreetly wipe your nose with a tissue. Don't blow! This will save you from a lot of disgusted glances.

Leave Maiko and Geisha alone:

It's become a popular thing to post selfies with Maiko or Geisha all over the internet but think of how those selfies were taken. Tourists would often harass these people and make them stop and take a selfie with them. This may seem like all fun and games. It may seem like the perfect photo opportunity. However, it is extremely rude and selfish to do this. Maiko and Geisha are not dressing up like this for fun or to look good. This is their job. They run around in these outfits all day, from place to place, so they can do their job. By insisting that they stop and take a selfie with you, you are putting their livelihood at risk because they may end up being late to an engagement. This is considered to be unacceptable behavior in Japan, so just don't do it.

If you really want that selfie though, there are fake Maiko or Geisha who are happy to take a picture with you. You'll know the difference because they won't be in a hurry. They'll be strolling down the street at a leisurely pace. They will be more than happy to take a selfie with you and no one will know the difference.

Don't Jaywalk:

This is true in most countries; however, in Japan, the rules are followed and the laws are obeyed, even the small ones. In Japan, it is not only against the law to jaywalk; it is also very dangerous. Some believe that it is so unacceptable to jaywalk because of how trusting the people in Japan are. If they're standing in a large crowd on the side of the road and someone decides they're going to run across the road before the green walking light turns on, then someone who isn't paying attention might see them out of the corner of their eye and assume it is safe to walk as well. If multiple people walk because they see one person jaywalking and assume the light is on, then you have a lot of people blocking up the road and nearly getting hit by speeding vehicles. This may or may not happen, but it's safer just to do what everyone else is doing and follow the law. The walkways and traffic lights in Japan are very good so you don't need to worry about not being able to cross the street.

Don't Use Your Phone in Areas of Respect:

When visiting shrines, temples, and other areas of respect, remember to turn your phone on silent or turn it off altogether. These places are places of worship. You wouldn't be taking phone calls and playing on your phone in a church, would you? Be mindful of those around you. They may be praying or paying their respects. They don't want to hear your phone's ringtone or that ding every time you get a message. Also, restrain yourself from snapping photos or selfies while in these places. This is also seen as rude.

Watch What You Wear:

This may seem obvious, but when visiting another country, it's always good to have a look at what the locals wear. You don't have to dress in any traditional Japanese clothing. However, you can have a look at what is expected of people in public. For instance, in Japan, the women dress more conservatively. They don't show their shoulders or chest area, but it is acceptable for them to wear really short shorts for some reason. As a tourist, you won't be punished for showing off your shoulders, but it's still good to have a look at what everyone is wearing so you can try to blend in. No one wants to stick out.

In cities like Tokyo, the Japanese like to dress smartly, but you can get away with smart casual if you are looking to blend in.

Try to avoid wearing any active wear while out on the streets. If you're going hiking in one of the many hiking destinations in Japan, then active wear is acceptable. However, if you wear that on the streets in the city, you will definitely stand out.

If you're pregnant, then consider getting some loose-fitting dresses or shirts. In Japan, sporting a baby bump with some tight clothing is frowned upon.

Keep the dress code in mind when putting on your shoes. Remember that in most places you will be required to remove your shoes before entering. It's better to wear easy to remove shoes, like sandals. If you don't want to walk around barefoot, then you may want to consider bringing some socks in your bag if you aren't wearing any.

Book and Purchase Things in Advance:

This is a must if you are visiting Japan. Not only will it save you from lots of stress but it's also the polite thing to do. You can't walk up to a hotel or an event in Japan and expect them to accommodate you at the last minute. It's better for every party involved that you book and pay for things in advance.

Hang on to Your Trash:

Japan is an exceptionally clean and litter-free country. Their streets are so clean that you will be surprised. However, there are very few bins to be found anywhere on the street. The Japanese value cleanliness and so they hang on to their trash and throw it out when they get home or to their work. It's a good idea to bring a bag with you so that you can keep your trash in it. There usually isn't any need for bins to be scattered around the streets because people don't walk and eat or drink as mentioned before. All of the bins can be found in those few places where you can sit down and eat or in the smoking areas. Don't be the tourist that litters – hang on to your trash.

Keep on the Left:

In Japan, everyone stays to the left. You'll be surprised to learn that Japan is one of the few countries where cars drive on the left. Pedestrians and bikers also tend to keep to the left on the streets. It's quite the sight to see. Everyone naturally walks to one side, so you don't end up running into or pushing past someone while on the streets. You'll see the same thing happen when exiting and entering elevators and staircases. It's best to notice the flow of the traffic and go with it. Just keep to the left and you'll be fine.

Be Kind to the Nara and Miyajima Deer:

On Nara and Miyajima Island, the deer residents have become popular tourist attractions. Their growing popularity has come with some problems. Some of the tourists don't respect the deer and this leads to some deer-related injuries. It is okay to take some pictures of the deer, but luring them towards you with a treat only to remove it and take a quick photo is not a good idea. This will annoy the deer and their annoyance will lead to them kicking, ramming, or biting you. Remember that these islands are not just tourist attractions; they are sacred places. It doesn't hurt to be respectful of the island and the deer living there.

Don't feed the deer human food. Buy some deer food from a vendor and don't wait too long before giving the food to the deer. This is the equivalent of teasing a dog, which we are all taught not to do. Remember that these are wild animals and they can hurt you.

Learn Some Basic Japanese:

This is a given. Tourists in a new country are not required to learn to speak the language fluently, but it doesn't hurt to learn a few words and phrases. This is convenient for all parties involved. You can avoid the annoyance of trying to explain yourself to someone who doesn't speak English and you can avoid annoying the Japanese person who has no idea what you're trying to say no matter how much you gesture or how slowly you talk. Most of the Japanese will understand some basic English, but you can also help the situation by learning some basic Japanese. A bonus is you get to see how happy you make someone when they hear you speak their language. Being so considerate is highly admired in Japan.

Public Transportation:

It is highly recommended that you use public transportation during your trip to Japan. There are some places where you can hire a car, but you shouldn't. In Japan, they drive on the left, as mentioned, and this is easy to forget for some tourists. The number of tourists in hired car accidents has risen over the years. Japan's public transportation system is highly advanced and very reliable. A trip to Japan is incomplete if you haven't taken advantage of the public transportation, of which there are three options: normal and highway buses, commuter or metro trains, and the Shinkansen (bullet trains). You will also need to know the etiquette that is expected of you while traveling on a train or a bus.

1. Entering the train

It is good manners to allow everyone exiting the train to leave before you get on it. Stand to the side and keep the area in front of the train doors clear. When everyone has finished leaving the train you can climb on. Do this in an orderly fashion as well. There may be a line of people waiting. Wait in the line and move as it does. Don't try to push past anyone to get on the train faster because this is rude and dangerous.

There's a specific way to queue in line for a train in Japan. There will be a thick and textured line right before the edge of the platform. The line will start behind this line. You will either be lining up in a single file or two by two. In some stations, there will be someone walking around making sure everyone is far enough away from the edge when the train is arriving or there will be a physical barrier with sliding doors.

2. Sitting on the train

On the trains, there will be priority seats on both ends of each car. These seats are reserved for the elderly, disabled, and pregnant. Do not sit in these seats if you don't qualify. Some trains will have female-only cars to protect women from sexual harassment during busy hours. These cars will be marked by a pink sign. There will also be marked lines on the seats. This is to show the amount of space you are expected to take up. Refrain from taking up more space than you are supposed to as the trains usually get really busy and there should be enough space for everyone. Keep your feet flat on the floor and close to you so you don't take up space in the aisle. If there are no seats, do not sit on the floor as this will cause an obstruction.

3. Be Quiet

When on a train you will be surrounded by lots of people and you should be considerate. This means that you shouldn't talk loudly on your phone, listen to loud music, and you should put your phone's volume on silent if you're receiving messages. In fact, if you can, just be quiet.

4. No Eating, Drinking, or Smoking

Not smoking on a train is a pretty obvious rule, but you shouldn't eat or drink either. Some trains do allow their passengers to eat on the train but it's better not to do this as you may upset some of your fellow passengers. Food and drink can sometimes have a strong smell. In small spaces with no windows that strong smell is made even stronger. Be considerate and avoid food, drink, and smoking while on a public train. There may be designated smoking cars on some of the trains, so look out for that if you want to smoke.

5. Take What You Brought onto the Train Off:

Just like when you're walking around, you don't want to leave your litter lying about. There won't be any bins inside the train. Don't leave anything behind. Whatever you bring on to the train, take it off with you when you leave. Don't leave your trash or litter behind. This is just good manners.

6. Keep Moving

When it gets really busy people are in a rush to get on to the train. To prevent getting in anyone's way or having people push past you, just keep moving. When you enter the train, move as far back on the train as you can. This will prevent you from stopping in the middle of the car and having people push past you. Move until there is no one else coming onto the train and the rush has stopped. Then you can stop and look for a seat.

7. Baggage Storage

Most buses, commuter trains, and the Shinkansen (bullet trains) will have overhead luggage racks. You can store your backpacks and bulky luggage up there. This will ensure that you aren't taking up too much space. If there isn't any place to put your luggage, then keep it on your lap, underneath your seat, or close to your feet. The goal here is to take up as little space as possible and not to cause an obstruction.

8. Reserved Seats

Some buses and trains may have reserved seats on them. Highway buses in Japan usually have reserved seats and you should only sit in your seat. Your seat number will be marked on your ticket. The Shinkansen usually also has reserved seating as well as non-reserved seating. The car number, seat row, and seat number will be marked on your ticket. Make sure you sit in the right seat and in the right car if you have a reserved ticket. If you don't, then find a non-reserved car and sit in any empty seat as long as it is not a priority seat.

9. Leaving the Train

Leaving the train is simple but you have to be ready for it. If you know that your stop is coming next, start making your way towards the exit ahead of time. People will see that you are moving towards the exit and they will move out of your way. Be sure to do the same for others. Move out of the train in an orderly fashion and try not to push into or past anyone. The Japanese tend to move quickly and smoothly so it shouldn't take too long for you to leave the train. Just be patient, wait your turn, and be considerate to others. Remember that those trying to board the train are waiting for you to leave before they can. Don't make them wait too long.

Chapter 5

Praise and Criticism

Praising someone on a job well done or a meal well-made is seen as the right and polite thing to do in almost any society. A compliment can go a long way. You can make someone smile, you can make them feel confident, and you can make their day just that much better. However, in Japan, it's a whole different story.

Unlike what most people might think, the strict manners and etiquette taught to children at a young age are not done so with the threat of harsh punishment. If a child makes a mistake, it is okay. If they get it right, they are praised to the ninth degree. This is the way they teach children all of the different manners, customs, and ways of life expected of them. However, this only lasts for so long. Once the children start to get older, the praise and compliments start to lessen. This is because once they get older, these things are expected of them and simply bowing the correct way is not seen as worthy of praise because it is expected.

This extends into all forms of adult life in Japan. Praising someone or giving them a compliment has become a minefield. The reason for this is the group ethic in Japan. There are no individuals in Japan, only members of groups. If you are given a compliment or praised for something like your talent or your beauty, then you are immediately singled out as an individual. This damages the group. In some cases, this can lead the person to be ostracized from the group and they will no longer be welcomed by them. Usually, if someone is to be praised for their talents, it is the group that must be praised as well.

The Japanese are known for their humbleness and this is what ends up saving them socially. If the star player on a sports team is too cocky or is given too much praise by the coach, he may end up being ostracized by the rest of the team. Instead, the player must be humble and insist that his skill is no good without the skill of the rest of the team.

If compliments and praise are to be given, it is best to do so privately. This is also better for such instances as when you wish to compliment a lady on her appearance. If you have no other option but to praise someone in public, you can do so in a more indirect way. Instead of telling someone that they are very talented, say "I wish I had talent like you." This is a way to compliment someone without setting him apart from the group or disgracing the group.

Criticism is a far different game to play with its own obstacles. The Japanese are extremely sensitive to criticism and for good reason. Throughout their history, any mistake or incorrect behavior could lead to shame for themselves and their family. This meant that any kind of criticism can be seen as an act of shaming. The shame felt by these individuals was so bad that the only way to set things right was through revenge or suicide. If justice was unattainable by revenge, then suicide was the only other option.

You may have witnessed it in a few movies where a samurai had brought such shame to himself and his family that suicide was the only way to right his wrong. You can rest assured that any criticism you give will not be bad enough to make someone kill themselves. However, since this is such a sensitive area in Japan, it would be better to avoid criticizing someone at all. Even if they are well deserving of criticism, it is best for everyone if you just avoid it.

A safe option is to bring up your troubles with a third party, perhaps someone older or of a higher ranking. Bring it up to them in an indirect way. They will probably know how to handle this kind of situation and they can sort the problem out. Otherwise, it is better to leave it alone.

Chapter 6

Visiting Shrines and Temples

In Japan, you will find plenty of temples and shrines to visit. There are at least a thousand Buddhist temples and Shinto shrines. Some of the shrines and temples can be dated back over 2000 years and are known for the important roles they played in Japan's history. These places have become major attractions for both foreigners and locals. The shrines and temples receive over a million visitors every year.

In Japanese the Buddhist temples are called o'tera, which is pronounced oh-tay-rah. A Buddhist temple is usually marked by a very large, ornate gate. These gates are usually mistaken for being the temple by tourists, but they are generally placed just a short distance from the actual temple. In front of the temple, you will find a long line of incense burners. Beside those are usually stalls where visitors to the temple can purchase some incense for themselves.

In Japanese, the Shinto shrines are called jinja, which is pronounced jeen-jah. The most distinguishing part of a Shinto shrine is its gate, or torii, pronounced toe-ree. The torii stands in front of the shrine and has become a worldwide known symbol for Japan. The torii is unique in structure and it is made up of two upright pillars with two crossbeam's right at the top. The torii serves a function. It sets the boundary for the shrine and signifies to visitors that once they pass the gate they are in a sacred place and must behave as such. Usually, the larger the shrine and its surrounding grounds are, the larger the torii is. You will usually find two or three more torii over the pathway leading up to the shrine. In ancient times, the moment you walked through the first torii, you would be silent and respective. Nowadays, the shrines have been turned into a tourist site. Just beyond the first torii gate, you will find rows or shops, which completely destroy the tranquility side of visiting a shrine in Japan. However, after the next toriis, the tranquility will return as you enter the shrine.

At the entrance to the shrine, there are usually two stone statues. They look like a pair of dogs and are called Koma-inu, which is pronounced koh-mah-eenuu. One of them will have its mouth closed and the other's mouth will be open. They are both slightly asymmetrical. The statues are there to guard each side of the shrine's entrance.

Both Buddhist temples and Shinto shrines will have various sizes. Some will be large with many different buildings used for meetings and prayer while others will be as small as a single altar where a deity is enshrined. The largest and most famous shrines and temples like the Meiji Shrine attract a lot of visitors from all over the country. Visiting a shrine or a temple in Japan has turned into a recreational outing rather than a religious visit. Even so, there are things you can and can't do while in a temple or a shrine. Some of these etiquette rules may seem like an obvious thing to you but some of them may surprise you. If you plan on visiting any shrines or temples, big or small, you should familiarize yourself with the proper etiquette expected of the visitors in these places.

Shinto Shrine Etiquette

You already know how to tell the difference between a Shinto shrine and a Buddhist temple. The differences don't just stop at their gates. There are also different mannerisms and etiquette for each one. Visiting a Shinto shrine is enjoyable, elegant, and tranquil as long as you know what you can and can't do while you're there.

Entering the Shrine:

Since the torii gate marks the start of the holy ground, it is not right for you to simply pass it as if it were a normal gate. Before passing underneath the torii, you should offer up a bow first. Once you have bowed, showing the deities your respect, then you can pass through the torii. When you walk through the torii, you should walk close to the left or right pillar and not in the middle. The middle of the entrance is holy ground where the gods walk so you should not walk there.

Most visitors to the shrines do not follow these rules for the entrance, but it is the correct and proper way to enter a Shinto shrine. This way, you won't offend anyone or any deity.

Purifying Ritual:

Upon entering the shrine, you will see a water fountain, also known as a chozuya. There will be ladles sitting on a central rest which is usually made from bamboo. The fountain is there so that visitors may wash themselves before entering the main hall or worshiping area of the shrine. This is a purifying ritual that is meant to purify both your body and your mind.

To perform the purifying ritual;

1. Take the ladle with your right hand and scoop some water onto your left hand. Then do the same the other way around.

2. Cup your hands and pour some water into them. Now sip up that water, swirl it about in your mouth, and spit it out onto the ground next to the fountain. Many people skip this step so you can if you want to. However, it is part of the ritual, so you don't have to skip it if you want to have the full experience.

After completing the ritual, you can move into the inner part of the shrine or the main half of worship, also known as the haiden, pronounced hi-dane.

Donations:

In the main hall, you will find a heavy rope hanging from the ceiling with a wooden box, or any other kind of box, underneath it. This is the donation box, and before you give a donation, you should know how to. You can't just put some money in it and walk away.

To give a donation:

1. As you approach the haiden you must offer up a slight bow and hold for a few seconds.

2. Throw your donation into the box, (you can be as generous as you want to be with your donation, but any donation is appreciated, even just a coin.)

3. After you've given your donation, you can pull the rope that rings the bell it is attached to. This is to call the gods and let them know you are there to pray. You only need to pull the rope once. In some shrines, there is no bell so you can skip this step.

4. Now you can offer up the prayer bow. You will bow deeply, like the respect bow explained earlier in this book; do this twice.

5. After rising from your second bow, clap your hands together twice.

6. Bow deeply one more time, the same as the respect bow but a bit deeper and hold it for a bit longer. You have completed the donation.

To excuse yourself from the donation box or the haiden if you want to leave, you can simply offer up a slight bow as you did when you approached the haiden.

Main Sanctuary:

In some shrines, you will find the main sanctuary, also known as the honden, pronounced hone-dane. This is where the spirit of the shrine's deity resides. You can come here to offer up extra prayer, but you don't have to if you're just a visitor. While photography may be permitted in the outer areas of the shrine and in the main hall of worship, it is usually prohibited in this area. There will be signs to show this. Make sure to keep a lookout for the signs and if you can't find any then stay on the safe side and keep the camera packed away.

Shoes or no shoes:

Some Shinto Shrines allow you to wear your shoes inside, but others may ask you to remove them at the door. To be sure, before you enter the shrine, have a look at the people inside. If they are wearing shoes, then you know it is okay. If they aren't and you see a line of shoes at the door then you know you need to remove yours as well. There may also be signs for you so be sure to check.

You can leave your shoes by the entrance, there's a good chance no one is going to steal them, or you can put them in your bag and carry them with you. To not seem untrusting and rude it is best if you leave your shoes at the door.

Obvious Rules:

Here are some obvious rules that probably aren't worth mentioning here, but I'll mention them anyway just in case.

1. No smoking while on shrine grounds. The moment you pass the torii you are on shrine grounds.

2. No eating or drinking while on shrine grounds.

3. Be silent and respectful while on shrine grounds, especially within the main hall of worship and the main sanctuary.

4. Don't take photos of people during the purification ritual or during prayer. You are fully allowed to take photos of yourself while doing these things as long as you do it in a respectful manner. Others may not want you photographing them during their prayer so don't do it.

5. Look for signs and obey them all.

6. Do not linger or stare while someone is praying.

7. Do not block entrances or hallways.

8. Do not linger or take your time during the purification ritual or while giving a donation.

9. Do always perform the purification ritual every time you visit.

10. Do always give a donation every time you visit, even if it is just a small one.

Buddhist Temple Etiquette

The rules and etiquette that are expected of you at a Buddhist temple are similar to that expected of you at a Shinto shrine.

Entering a Temple:

The rules for entering the Buddhist temple are similar to those of entering a Shinto shrine, but there are a few differences. The entrance to the temple, also known as a sanmon is more ornate than the torii gates and it actually looks like a small house. However, this is not the entrance to the actual temple, but it is the entrance to the temple grounds.

You do not have to bow before passing through these gates, but you should walk near to the left or right and not in the middle. Once again, the middle is considered to be holy ground where the gods walk, so don't walk there.

Incense Ritual:

Right before the entrance to the actual temple, you'll find rows of incense burners or a big metal pot with an incense holder in the middle and ash from the incense in the bottom. There will also be stalls where you can buy some incense, or you can bring your own. You don't have to perform this ritual before entering the temple, but it is part of the experience and shows more respect.

1. Light the incense, whether you buy it from the stalls or bring your own, it doesn't matter.

2. Traditionally you should wave the incense smoke around your body once you've lit it. This will cleanse and purify your mind.

3. Place the incense in the incense burner. This is basically an offering to the gods before you pray.

That is the end of the ritual, now you can enter the temple.

Inside the Temple:

The inside of the temples is usually similar to the inside of the shrines. There will be a chozuya as you approach the main temple. You should purify yourself at the water fountain before entering. This is why you can skip the incense outside because you will be purifying yourself here.

The purification ritual in the temple is the same as the one in the shrine. You can also skip the final spitting out the water step if you want.

The rest of the temple will be arranged the same way or in a similar way. There will be a donation box, but you won't have to do the whole bowing ritual.

Worshiping at the Temple:

The rituals for praying at the temples are similar to those of the shrines but with less bowing and no clapping. You simply put your hands together while praying. So during the donation box ritual, you should just put your hands together instead of clapping them and there is no need to bow.

No Shoes:

At Buddhist temples, you will have to remove your shoes at the entrance. There will be shelves or lines to place your shoes in or you will be given a plastic bag to carry your shoes around in. It's very rare that a temple won't ask you to remove your shoes, but if you're not sure, there will probably be signs.

Obvious Rules:

These obvious rules will be pretty similar to those above, but I'll mention them again just in case.

1. No smoking, eating, or drinking on the temple grounds.

2. The moment you pass through the gate onto the temple grounds, you should be silent and respectful.

3. No photography inside the temple itself. You will usually be allowed to take photos outside the temple and inside the gate but not inside the temple.

4. Don't linger or stare while people are praying.

5. Don't linger or take your time at the incense burner, water fountain, or donation box.

6. Don't block entrances or hallways.

7. Turn your phone off and make no loud noises, unless you can't help it like sneezing or coughing.

8. Look out for signs and obey them.

With that, you know everything you need to know about visiting a Shinto shrine or Buddhist temple while in Japan. Remember that while these are tourist locations, they are also sacred sites and places of worship. All you really need to do is be respectful to the grounds, the deities, and the worshipers there.

Make sure to visit all of the stalls and shops you'll find on the outside of the shrines and temples. Most of these are selling things in exchange for donations for the temple or shrine. Something that you must do while in Japan is purchase an Ema. This is meaning "horse picture" and it is a wooden plaque you can purchase and hang on the grounds. You scribble on the plague all of your hopes and wishes for the coming year and hang it on the grounds of the temple or shrine. It is believed that the deities will read your plague and, if you were respectful enough during your visit to their shrine or temple, they will work to make your hopes and wishes come true. This and plenty more things can only add to the experience when you visit the temples and shrines.

Chapter 7

Visiting Another's Home

Visiting someone's home in Japan has its very own set of rules. You may already know of some from watching movies and shows on television. The one rule everyone knows is to remove your shoes before you enter someone else's home, but did you know that there will be house slippers for you to wear while inside the house? Do you know about bathroom slippers? There are a considerable amount of rules but they're all just basic manners at the end of the day. They're simple to learn and easy to remember.

Arriving:

You should always arrive on time if you are invited to someone's home. It may be acceptable for Westerners to arrive just before the time or a little after it but not in Japan. They admire punctuality. You should try to arrive as close to the time you're supposed to. Too early or even a little late is seen as rude and disrespectful. You're better off arriving a little early than late at all.

Don't Invite Anyone:

If you are invited to someone's home, then that's it. You're invited, no one else. If you want to invite someone to come with you then you should ask your host first if it is okay. If they are alright with it then you can invite someone. If they aren't, then deal with it. If the host is okay with it and you do invite someone that your host doesn't know you must introduce them properly and politely. Make sure they are aware of the customs and etiquette before inviting them.

Announcing Your Arrival:

When you arrive at someone's home in Japan, knock on the door or ring the doorbell and then wait patiently until someone answers. Don't ring the doorbell too frequently or knock too loudly. Wait a respectable amount of time before knocking or ringing again if no one answers.

When someone answers the door, you should greet them with a smile, a bow of the right amount of respect, and say "ojama shimasu." This means "Sorry for intruding or disturbing you." It is polite to say this whenever someone opens the door to you. It is humble and shows you are grateful and respectful towards the host for all the trouble they went through to have you over.

Bring a Gift:

Whenever you are invited to someone's home it is customary to bring them a gift. The gift doesn't have to be expensive or extravagant, but it should be wrapped properly and presented in the proper way.

Acceptable gifts:

1. Basket of fruit

2. Cookies

3. Cake

4. Bottle of wine or whiskey (particularly for men)

5. Coffee

6. Candy

7. Flowers (tread carefully what flowers you bring)

When handing the gift to your host, smile kindly, bow your head slightly, and say "tsumaranai mono desu ga." This means "It's nothing special but here is a little something for you." This is a humble way of giving your gift. It is polite, shows that you are grateful, and doesn't make it look like you are making a big deal or showing off that you bought them a gift.

Shoes and Slippers:

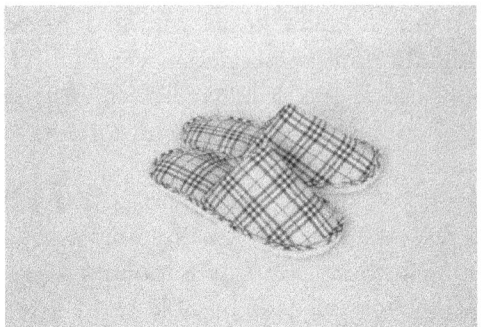

When entering a home, you should always remove your shoes. You may not be asked to but that is because it is a must that everyone knows to do. The entrance to the home will have a lowered floor called a genkan. This is where you remove and place your shoes. Some people make the mistake of removing their shoes on the raised floor and placing them on the lowered floor. This is wrong. Your shoes should never touch the raised floor. Step into the genkan, remove your shoes, place them neatly beside the other shoes there facing towards the door. This is polite and also makes it easier to put your shoes back on when you are leaving. Try to wear socks or stockings. This is more polite than just being barefoot.

Some homes will have slippers for you to wear inside the home. Some do not have slippers so keep this in mind. If you see others are wearing slippers and there are slippers available then, by all means, put them on. There may also be bathroom slippers for you to use in the bathroom. You'll find them by the bathroom door. Put them on while you're in the bathroom and switch back to your house slippers when you're done. When you leave, make sure to place the slippers back as neatly as you found them.

Sitting:

After all of the meeting and the greeting is done, the host will probably show you to the room where they will be entertaining. This will probably be the dining room or living room. There will be plenty of seats and some people may already be sitting down. It is better that you remain standing and wait for your host to show you where you should sit. It is impolite to just take any seat that you want.

During Mealtime:

If you have been invited over to eat a meal, then it is best to stick to the manners and etiquette you'll find in the eating and dining area of this book. Some people may have their own customs they follow in their house. Try to be observant and watch others so you can learn these customs.

Generally, you should compliment the chef, which may be your host, by saying "umai" or "oishii" during the meal. If you love the food but you keep quiet and don't express it in any way, then the chef or host may think that you do not like the food.

If you don't like a certain food and don't want to eat it just be polite about it. You don't have to pretend to like it or keep quiet and avoid it. Just say politely that you aren't a big fan of that particular food. There's no need to pretend, but you should also avoid acting too negatively.

After Mealtime:

When the meal is done and everyone has finished eating, the host may begin clearing up and cleaning straight away. If they do, then you should offer to help. The host will probably insist that you don't need to help them and that you should just relax and get to know the other guests. Even if the host rejects your offer, it is still a very polite gesture. They will thank you for it even if they don't want you to help and you'll definitely earn yourself some positive points.

While the host is cleaning up, you can take the opportunity to sit and socialize with the other guests. During this time, you may consider complimenting the décor of the house or talk about how good the food was. This is the perfect way to compliment the host without directly doing so. They'll hear about it from the other guests or even hear you from the other room while they're cleaning. It's all about being a good guest and making sure the host feels as if they have done a great job. You can also try to make small talk with the other guests. Be careful what you talk about as you don't want to risk offending or angering another guest. Allow the other guests to take lead with the small talk and let them choose the topic of conversation.

Leave:

After everything is said and done it is best not to overstay your welcome. In some countries, it is considered rude if you leave a party too early, but in Japan, you really shouldn't stay too late. After a good meal you may want to lie back, put your feet up, and browse your phone, but don't do this. It will be seen as rude by your hosts and the other guests. You can stay and talk for a while after the meal. They may even invite you to have a few drinks with them, but avoid drinking too much. You don't want to get too drunk or over excited while at someone else's house. Even if the host or the other guests are acting this way remember that you are in some else's house and you should try to be as polite as possible.

When you do eventually leave, you can thank the host for having you over and for the great food and fun evening. Be as polite in your exit as you were in your entrance. You don't have to wait for another guest to 'break the ice' before you can leave. Simply state that it's getting late and you would like to leave. There's nothing wrong with that.

Visiting someone's home in Japan can be a great way to have a close look at their culture. It really is a part of the whole experience. Making sure that you follow all the correct etiquette and mannerisms while you're there will ensure that you are invited over again in the future.

Chapter 8

Bathroom Etiquette:

You may look at something like a bath or a toilet and think, "I know how to use that." You wouldn't think that different countries and cultures have their own dos and don'ts about using a bathroom. It should be universal right? Well no, it's not. Just like everything else in Japan, there is a certain etiquette when it comes to using public or private toilets and baths. Yes, there are public baths. Knowing the rules that come with using these things can make your life in Japan much easier.

Public Bathrooms

Finding Public Bathrooms

You know how to find a public toilet while you're out and about in other countries, but do you know how to find one in Japan? Will there be signs? Will I be able to find a toilet in this building? How do I ask someone where the toilet is? These are all the questions that you should be asking yourself. Here are the answers.

Signs:

In Japan, there will be several signs in public showing you where the public toilets are located. Buildings may also have signs showing you where the toilets are. Some of these signs will be the usual pictures you expect of a man, a woman, someone in a wheelchair, or even just a picture of a toilet. However, some of the signs will have the word for the toilet written instead.

Here are the many different words used to describe the toilet:

1. Senmenjo which means washroom

2. Toire which means toilet

3. Otearai which means bathroom

4. Keshoshitsu which means powder room

Asking Someone:

You can use the words mentioned above when asking someone where the toilets are or telling someone that you need to go to the bathroom. Be careful about which words you use during certain situations. For instance, when you are sitting down having a meal, you won't ask someone where the toire is. This is a direct translation to toilet, and you don't want to use that word while people around you are eating. Instead use the word senmenjo, which means washroom, or keshhoshitu, which means powder room.

There are polite and impolite words to use given different situations. If you are unsure which word to use just think to yourself, do I want to be thinking about a toilet or a bathroom in this situation? If you don't, then don't use those words. If you wouldn't mind, then chances are the people around you don't mind either. To be safe, just use the words for washroom or powder room instead of the words for toilet or bathroom. You may be able to get away with using the word for bathroom but tread carefully.

Buildings with Bathrooms:

If you're running around the streets looking for a bathroom but can't seem to find one, you can always look to the nearest building and hope they have a toilet. Some places will have access to the toilet but not for public use. You don't want to waste your time going into these places. There are obvious places that have toilets for public use such as airports, stations, shopping centers, tourist spots, parks, convenience stores, and lodgings. If you're in doubt as to where to find a toilet, just go to any place where tourists usually frequent. There will always be public toilets there.

Be aware that most restaurants will not let you use their toilets unless you are a customer. The same goes for some hotels. If you are not staying at the hotel then they probably won't let you use their toilets.

Types of Toilets and How to Use Them

There are three different types of toilets in Japan. They each have different functions and ways of using them. There are traditional Japanese toilets, also known as washiki toire. They have western-style toilets, which are the toilets most tourists will be familiar with, these are also known as yoshiki toire. Lastly, they have takino-toire, which are multifunction toilets.

You'll obviously know how to use a western-style toilet so I don't need to explain that, but the others will probably need some explaining.

Traditional Japanese Toilets:

These toilets are very different to normal western toilets that we know and use today. A traditional Japanese toilet is sunken into the ground and it requires the user to squat down while using it. It is shaped similarly to a modern urinal but in the floor.

To use a traditional Japanese toilet then you need to squat over it facing the head of the toilet where the lever to flush is. Do not face the opposite way. When you're done you can flush the toilet and leave.

You won't find these toilets in modern Japanese homes. They are most common in some old public bathrooms, some tourist attractions, and really old buildings.

Western-Style Toilets:

The Western-Style toilet is the most common toilet you'll find in Japan. It will be in most homes, hotels, public places like malls and convenience stores, and places like train stations and airports.

These toilets can be used in the same way you would use your own toilet. Some of the toilets will have a small sink area at the top. This sink has clean, recycled water that you can use to clean your hands when you're finished.

Multi-function Toilet:

You'll find these toilets in a larger room because they take up a lot more space than other toilets. This is so people in wheelchairs and people with children can use them. These toilets are prioritized for the disabled and for parents with children, but they can be used by anyone.

These are usually more digital and futuristic with lots of buttons to push and functions to take advantage of. All of the buttons can be overwhelming. If you're not sure what a button does, then you probably shouldn't push it. Some of these restrooms even have a button to press for emergencies, but those are usually for the elderly or disabled.

You don't have to use these toilets if you feel as though they may be too complicated for you. You can always opt for simpler Western-style or traditional Japanese toilets instead.

Public Bathroom Etiquette

1. Flush the toilets when you are finished.

2. Face the right direction on a traditional Japanese toilet.

3. Make sure not to squat on Western-style toilets.

4. Don't throw toilet paper into the trash bins. The trash bins are only used for diapers and other sanitary products. Toilet paper should be flushed down the toilet if you need to dispose of it.

5. Some public toilets will offer bathroom slippers for you to use so you don't track any dirt from outside in. Be polite and take off your shoes before entering the bathroom and put the provided slippers on. These slippers will be clean. If you feel uncomfortable wearing the slippers alone then consider wearing socks with your shoes or bring a spare pair of socks to put on just in case.

6. Make sure to leave the bathroom in the condition you found it. Don't leave trash around or leave the toilet unflushed. The public bathrooms in Japan are in particularly good condition because each individual citizen works to keep it that way. You should also do your part.

Private or Hotel Bathrooms

Hotel Bathrooms

Most hotels and lodgings bathrooms are separated. The toilet and hand basin will be in one room separated by a glass shower door. On the other side of the door is the shower and bath. The shower is placed directly next to the bath in between it and the door.

Some hotels have a unit bath, which is when the shower, bath, and toilet share the same room. The shower is usually located inside the bath and the toilet is next to it. The shower has to be used while standing in the bath and there is a shower curtain you can pull across to keep the water from splashing the rest of the room.

Private Bathrooms

You'll find that most private bathrooms in houses are separated. Some of the smaller, cheaper houses will have unit baths though. The layout of a private bathroom is similar to a hotel or lodgings bathroom and the rules for both will be pretty much the same.

Private or Hotel Bathroom Etiquette

1. Men should lift toilet seats up before using them.

2. The toilet seat should always be put down when you are finished and before flushing.

3. The bathroom should be kept clean and tidy.

4. Toilet paper should be flushed down the toilet and not thrown into the trash bin. Everything else needs to be put in the trash bin.

5. Bathroom slippers should always be worn in the bathroom and nowhere else in the house. House slippers or normal shoes should never be worn in the bathroom. This will help keep the bathroom hygienic.

6. When leaving the bathroom, place the slippers to the side of the door with the toes facing the bathroom door. This will make it easier for the next person to use them.

7. Close the bathroom door while showering or bathing as the steam can sometimes set off the smoke alarm in some hotels.

Bathing and Showering in Japan

Bathing in Japan is seen as a form of relaxation and leisure, where showering is seen as a method of cleaning yourself. While in Japan you should never clean yourself in the bath. This is why in most bathrooms the shower is placed beside the bath and in its own separate room.

It is believed that soap should never touch your bath water and one should be as clean as possible when they enter a bath. Therefore, one should always shower and clean themselves before getting into a bath. If you have a unit bath, where your shower is in the bath, then you will have to clean the bath after you shower before you can use it. This is to make sure there is no dirt or soap residue left behind after your shower.

Bathing and Showering Etiquette

1. Shower and wash yourself properly before a bath.

2. Women or men with long hair should tie their hair up before getting into the bath.

3. You should never dunk your head in the water while bathing.

4. You should never bath while you are dirty.

5. Clean the bath and shower thoroughly before and after use.

6. Usually, a small cloth is given to you to use in the bath, but this should not be put in the bath water. You can put this on your head or leave it on the side.

7. Always dry yourself properly before stepping into the bathroom slippers.

Chapter 9

Staying at Hotels:

When visiting Japan, you will most likely be staying in a hotel, inn, or lodging of some kind. You'll probably be spending a lot of time in and out of the place where you're staying. For that simple reason, it is important you know some of the simple dos and don'ts of staying at these places.

I would recommend staying at a Ryokan during your visit to Japan. These are old, traditional Japanese hotels whose customs date back to the Edo period. They are far less strict though. These hotels add to the whole Japanese experience and are great for a relaxing and fun filled time. If you are going to stay at a Ryokan hotel, then there are a few things you should know first.

Arrive on Time:

A Ryokan hotel is very precise about what time its guests arrive. If you book a room at the hotel and say you're going to be checking in at a certain time, then that is what they are going to expect. There will be a host of people waiting to greet and welcome you to the hotel, including chefs waiting to serve you some traditional cuisine. If you're going to be late or early, it is considerate to call ahead and warn the hotel.

No Shoes in the Rooms:

At this point, this will come as no surprise to you. The rooms in the hotel will have tatami mat floors and shoes should never be worn on these floors. There will be house slippers for you to wear during your stay, along with bathroom slippers, or you can walk around barefoot.

The Tea is Free:

Most of these hotels will have a selection of tea along with traditional tea cups and a teapot for you to use. The tea and the rice crackers, or other snacks with it, are all complimentary. The supply is refilled every day.

Your Bed:

When you first enter your room, you may notice that there is no bed or even a futon. Don't freak out. Staff will come to your room around dinner time or just after and lay out a futon for you to sleep on. This may seem odd, but it means that you have more room to walk around and have guests during the day. The same staff will come to your room and remove the futon after you are done using it for the day.

No Tipping:

There is no need to tip any of the hotel staff – not the waitresses, the chefs, or the people who clean your room or bring your futon to you. They find it insulting that you would offer them money for doing what they are expected to do. Therefore, keep that money in your pocket. A humble thank you is enough for them.

Tokonoma:

Almost every guest room in these traditional Japanese hotels will have a room called a tokonoma. These rooms are purely decorative. They will be well designed with some artwork, a scroll or two, maybe even a bonsai tree or ornate flowers. This room should be kept empty at all times. Do not store anything in here. Some guests make the mistake of storing their suitcases in this room but that is the worst thing you could do with them. This room should be enjoyed and admired, not filled with junk.

Yukata:

Every guest will be given a yukata. This is basically a black, fragile gown you can wear in the evening. It is acceptable for you to wear this while walking through the hotel and dining area as long as you wear it properly. Most guests will try to wear them loose but you should wear it tight and close to your neck. There should only be a small bit of your neck showing. You can use the cotton belt that comes with it to tighten it.

Do not take this home with you. This belongs to the hotel and is not complimentary. This may seem obvious to some people, but the hotels still have problems with guests leaving with their yukata.

The yukata should be folded and placed back in the cupboard when you leave the hotel and when you're not wearing it. It should never be placed on the floor.

Those are the basic things you need to know about staying at a hotel in Japan. These are the more traditional hotels and you won't find things like futons or tatami mat floors in more modern hotels. Staying in these hotels during your visit is the best option as it will give you the full Japanese experience. There really isn't that much to it, as long as you follow these simple rules and the rest of the etiquette tips, dos, and don'ts in the rest of this book.

Chapter 10

Japanese Ceremonies and Festivals

In Japan, there are many ceremonies and festivals to be attended throughout the year. One year in Japan is characterized by the four passing seasons. Every month in Japan is host to its own festival marking a new stage of the year. Some of the festivals are ancient traditions and some have shown up more recently. Aside from the different festivals, the tea ceremony is quite a popular one. It is riddled with rules, customs, and etiquette though and it would be fairly easy for a newcomer to make a mistake. Fear not, because this book is here to make sure you know what you need to know.

Japanese Festivals

There can be easily over 200 festivals in Japan in a year. Some of them are big and important like the matsuri festivals which are embedded in Japanese culture. This can either be big and loud or small and peaceful. Then there are small, not as important festivals like the coming of age festival or the cherry blossom festivals. These may not be as important, but the Japanese still celebrate them.

The following are the most major festivals:

1. The Gion Festival and the Aomori Nebuta Festival

These two festivals are the two major ones out of many small festivals held in summer, between June and August. These two festivals are the only major ones and they offer up a window into traditional Japan.

2. Kakunodate Cherry Blossom Festival and the Hirosaki Cherry Blossom Festival

These two are quite a sight to behold and should be part of any trip to Japan. They are held in spring and usually you will have to go to a Shinto shrine to attend.

3. Tokyo Motor Show, Tokyo International Film Festival, and the Tokyo Comic Con

These are some of the major events that are held in fall. As you can tell from the names, they are all held in Tokyo. They are not the only major events in fall, but they are the only ones held in Tokyo. They aren't very traditional in Japanese culture, but they are enjoyable.

4. Kawagoe Festival and the Fujiwara Autumn Festival

These festivals are also held in fall and they should not be missed. They are responsible for filling the country with colorful and historical parades. You can enjoy seasonal food and performances while attending this parade. They are a must-see.

5. Nozawa Fire Festival and the Sapporo Snow Festival

These are held in winter among others, but these festivals are the ones that attract thousands of people every year. Winter in Japan is actually quite a wonderful sight. Snow festivals are everywhere and people carve their favorite anime characters, political figures, historical figures, and other beautiful pieces into the ice and snow. You'll also find paths lit by white lanterns and lined with igloos.

These are the major or not to be missed festivals held in Japan throughout the year. There are plenty more for you to visit if you want, but they are either small festivals or just more of the same. Most Japanese festivals are very similar in what they contain:

1. Festival Music

Most, if not all, of the festivals are accompanied by music usually played from loud speakers. During some festivals, there will be a live performance where someone will sing along with a band consisting of bamboo flutes, drums, and bells. Most of the parades will have floats featuring dozens of singers and bands. Festivals that don't have music will generally have plenty of chanting to fill the silence.

2. Yatai Stalls

Another common thing in festivals are 'yatai' selling food, soft drinks, beer, and even some toys and games. The food they sell is usually based on the season and the type of festival. These are always present during the festivals.

There aren't many rules or proper etiquette to follow for any specific festival. The behavior for these is the usual social mannerisms and public etiquette people expect from you every day. There isn't anything in particular you need to do, say, or wear. You just need to know what the festival is about, where it is being held, and enjoy it.

Japanese Tea Ceremony

The Japanese Tea Ceremony is the height of formality, tradition, and hospitality in Japan. It is known as sado or chado, which is translated as "the way of tea." This tradition goes far back in Japanese history. It is a wonderful ceremony and even foreigners are given the opportunity to take part in one. During the ceremony, you gather with others in a quiet, calming, and tranquil environment and drink green tea. Usually, the ceremony is held in a traditional Japanese tea room with a tatami floor. In modern Japan, the ceremony is practiced as a hobby and not just a traditional way of life.

The protocol of a tea ceremony is precise, down to the specific hand movements one makes while handling the tea bowl. Tourists are of course not expected to know in detail these precise protocols. However, knowing the basic structure and rules of a tea ceremony can make the process much more enjoyable and smoother for everyone.

Tea Ceremony Etiquette:

The few steps you need to take and things you need to know will ensure you can enjoy the full experience of a traditional Japanese Tea Ceremony. A formal ceremony usually lasts for multiple hours. It starts with a meal, then a bowl of thick tea, and the ceremony usually ends with a second bowl of thin tea. Nowadays, most ceremonies are a bit shorter with just the drinking of the thin tea. This is most likely the ceremony you will attend and not the full, formal one.

What to Wear:

The Tea Ceremony is supposed to be relaxed and calming. You should avoid wearing flashy, uncomfortable, distracting clothes. Rather wear casual, plain, and comfortable clothes. Don't wear jewelry, especially on your wrists or fingers as this could damage the tea bowl. Don't wear any strong perfume. Don't wear anything that could distract from the smell of the tea or the calm, relaxing environment.

Washing Your Hands:

Traditional tea rooms are surrounded by a calm and tranquil garden. Many of the modern tea rooms available to tourists won't have a garden, but they will probably have a traditional stone basin near the entrance. Visitors to the tearoom should wash their hands in the stone basin before entering.

Entering the Tearoom:

The tearoom is generally a tatami room. The entrance is supposed to be low so that guests have to stay low to walk through. This is so the guests demonstrate humility upon entering the ceremony. The tearoom is usually decorated for the occasion, but you shouldn't stop and admire the decorations upon first entering the room.

Shoes are of course removed before entering the room. There may be slippers for you to wear, and if not, then your socks will do. Try to have clean socks on your feet or at least have a pair with you as you don't want to be barefoot for the ceremony.

The guest of honor or the highest on the social ranking bows to the host and enters the room. This guest will take the seat that is closest to the alcove in the room. The other guests follow, all bowing to the host upon entering, and take their seats in order. If you are unsure where to sit, someone will guide you to your place.

You will have to sit in the seiza position, remember that women lower into this position with both knees at once and men take one knee at a time, on the tatami floor. Once everybody is seated it is expected that you bow one last time before observing the decorations in the room.

Tea Preparation:

Traditionally the host prepares the tea in front of the guests, so this will be enjoyable to watch. This is a delicate task that requires precise action. Every piece of equipment was carefully selected for this exact occasion and they all have their proper place and proper way of being handled. You may watch the tea preparation, but make sure not to do anything that will distract from the event. Do not make any loud noise and don't talk or ask any question. Simply sit silently and watch.

Japanese Sweet:

Usually, a traditional Japanese sweet is served before the tea. This treat is very sweet and is supposed to compliment the extreme bitterness of the tea you're about to drink. This sweet should be eaten before the tea is poured and served. If you're not sure if you're allowed to eat the sweet or how to eat it, simply look around and wait for someone else to do it. Watch how they do it and then copy them. If the room is filled with tourists and none of you know what to do then that's okay. You aren't expected to know everything about the culture or customs.

Drinking the Tea and Admiring the Bowl:

When the tea is ready, it will be placed on the tatami mat in front of a guest. The tea is usually prepared in one tea bowl that can easily fit in your hand. The one bowl is shared between all of the guests.

When it is your turn to drink, the bowl will be placed on the tatami floor in front of you with the front of the bowl facing you. Pick up the bowl with your right hand only and then place it in your left hand. Using your right hand turn the bowl so the front of it is no longer facing you. Turning it clockwise about 90 degrees should be fine. If the front of the bowl isn't facing you when it is placed in front of you, then you don't have to worry about this.

Take a few slow, small sips from the bowl. You don't want to take a big sip as the bitterness will be quite strong. Take only a few sips then place it back on the tatami mat in front of you. Make sure that when you return the bowl to the mat the front of it is facing the one who prepared the tea. You should bow to the tea preparer after finishing drinking the tea and when you place the tea bowl in front of you. This is to show gratitude towards them for making the tea and allowing you to drink it.

At the end of the ceremony, there will be enough time for you to lift and admire the tea bowl. You should try to admire it as this is a part of the tea ceremony. The tea bowl was most likely carefully selected for this specific occasion. It is standard to admire and appreciate the delicate design, the effort that went into making it, and the thought that went into choosing it for this occasion. Don't admire it for too long or too short a time. Allow other guests enough time to also admire the bowl.

Ending the Ceremony:

Once everyone has finished admiring the tea bowl, it is placed back on the tatami mat with the front facing the host. The host will return it to the floor in front of them. They will then ask if anyone wants a second round of tea. If no one does, then the ceremony will end. The host will then begin cleaning the equipment and return them to where they were when the ceremony started. If someone wants a second round, then they will prepare some more tea and the ceremony will repeat.

At the end of the ceremony, it is customary to stand when everyone else does and bow one last time to the host and thank them before you leave.

A Few Rules:

1. The tea ceremony is a relaxing and tranquil experience, so remain quiet and attentive throughout the whole ceremony.

2. Always wash your hands in the stone basin before entering the tearoom. Do not skip this step.

3. Wipe the tea bowl after you have drunk the tea and before placing it back on the tatami mat. There will be a cloth by your seat that you can use.

4. Smile, be grateful, be kind, and always bow to the host upon receiving and after drinking from the tea bowl. This is a form of thanks and you should not give verbal thanks as this will break the silence.

Conclusion

I know it might seem overwhelming and unnecessary to have to follow all of these rules and regulations while away on holiday. Most people traveling to Japan are either there on vacation or for business. It's understandable that those there on vacation don't want to have to worry about etiquette and the right and wrong ways to do something. The best way to get past this is to look at the things in this book not as rules but as manners. That's all etiquette is at the end of the day. When visitors come into your country, you don't expect them to leave all of their manners behind; you expect them to follow your rules and etiquette. Of course, Japan expects the same.

I mentioned on several occasions in this book that most tourists are forgiven if they make mistakes or if they don't know how things are done. I mentioned also that showing the right behavior at the right time will make the locals love you. They don't expect you to know their customs, so it comes as a huge and great surprise to them when they see a tourist bow correctly instead of shaking hands.

The Japanese love tourists and they especially love tourists who know and understand their way of life. In my opinion, Japan is one of the greatest cultural places in the world. I would say that a visit to Japan should be on everyone's bucket list. No trip to Japan is complete without experiencing everything it has to offer, and that includes its etiquette and mannerisms.

Learning the things in this book will take you only a week and it will make your trip to Japan just that much better. For a full, traditional, and fun-filled experience, I suggest practicing the things in this book and putting them into full use during your trip. You won't be disappointed and neither will the locals.

Happy learning and enjoy your trip!

About Us

Welcome to JpInsiders, home of everything Japanese! If you're interested in the unique culture that this innovative and exciting country has to offer, we can offer you exactly what you're looking for and more.

Here at JpInsiders, we're experts in Japanese culture, and can satisfy your every need no matter what exciting area fascinates you.

Nestled in the heart of East Asia, Japan is home to one of the richest cultures the world has to offer, having pioneered an impressive range of concepts that have gained worldwide traction and popularity.

For example, Japan is the original home of anime and manga, the iconic Japanese cartoons and comic books that millions throughout the world have grown to know and love.

When it comes to the arts, Japan is forever developing new and exciting concepts. A whole host of popular crafts including bonsai, the art of growing miniature versions of trees or shrubs, and the intricate paper craft of origami both originated on Japanese soil.

Over the years, Japanese innovation has truly set a precedent that the rest of the world looks up to.

Whatever your personal interests, we are here to provide you with everything you may need to explore Japan's fascinating culture in greater detail.

We stock a range of books on everything from growing a bonsai tree to learning the Japanese language.

Or how about you get your hands on a great travel guide to help you pinpoint the must-see spots for your next visit?

Whether you are planning a memorable holiday in Japan, wishing to learn a brand-new skill, or simply intrigued by the country's wonderful culture, we will be delighted to help.

Explore our products and get ready to take in all the details you may like to know on Japanese culture.

If you have any question or query, please feel free to get in touch with us for more information. Immerse yourself in all the best and the most up-to-date details on this truly special country with the help of JpInsiders!

PS: Can I Ask You for a Quick Favor?

First of all, thank you for purchasing **Japanese Language & Culture**! I know that you could have picked any number of books to read, but you picked this one and for that I am extremely grateful.

If you enjoyed this book and found some benefit in reading it, I'd like to hear from you and hope that you could take some time to post a review if possible.

Your feedback and support will help me to greatly improve my writing craft for future projects and make this book even better.

THANKS!

=)

www.ingramcontent.com/pod-product-compliance
Lightning Source LLC
Chambersburg PA
CBHW071009080526
44587CB00015B/2403